D1226600

THE NEGLECTED
FACTOR

THE NEGLECTED
FACTOR

The ethical element in the Gospel

ERIC BAKER

ABINGDON PRESS

NEW YORK   NASHVILLE

The Cato Lecture of 1963

SET IN MONOTYPE IMPRINT AND PRINTED IN
GREAT BRITAIN BY COX AND WYMAN LTD
LONDON, FAKENHAM AND READING

PREFACE

THE opportunity of delivering the Fred J. Cato Lecture at the General Conference of the Methodist Church of Australasia is surely one of the greatest privileges any British Methodist can receive. When the Australasian Conference honoured me by their invitation, my gratitude was enhanced by the fact that, however unworthily, I was following in the footsteps of the late W. Russell Maltby, who was my minister in my formative years and who first put to me the challenge of the Christian Ministry.

Most of my brethren who have preceded me in the lectureship have published their lectures after the event, and have thus been able to express their appreciation of the generous kindness they have invariably received during their visit. At the request of the Australian friends, this volume is being prepared for publication at the time of the delivery of the lecture, but my own appreciation is no less sincere because of necessity it is expressed in anticipation.

It was part of the late Mr Cato's intention that, where possible, the lecturer should spend some considerable time in Australia, visiting all the States, and thereby help to cement the warm fellowship already existing between the Methodist Church in Australia and the mother Church in Great Britain. This is a most attractive prospect, and I look forward eagerly to the renewal of many existing friendships and the forming of new ones.

I would add one or two observations concerning the lecture itself. I am neither a professional theologian nor an original thinker. Of necessity, therefore, the lecture is addressed to the ordinary Christian in Australia and elsewhere, who is, I believe, as convinced as I am myself that Jesus Christ is the one hope of the world, and as concerned as I am at the apparent failure of the Churches to present the gospel in this present age with an effectiveness commensurate with the sincere and devoted efforts they make to do so.

Anything of value the lecture may contain is the passing on of what I have already received. While I am consciously or unconsciously indebted to many writers, my principal debt, which I gratefully acknowledge, is to the late John Oman. Those familiar with his book *Grace and Personality* will recognize the influence of his thought at many points in the ensuing pages. When I entered the Ministry, and for a considerable period afterwards, that book was required reading for Methodist probationers. Since that day, other schools of theological thought have dominated the scene, and the book has disappeared from the list. It would ill befit me to question the value of these later interpretations of the gospel, but in my judgement, nothing would equip the preacher of the gospel today more adequately for his difficult task than a return to the interpretation contained in that book. The events of the intervening years have only served to underline the significance and relevance of its approach, and I believe it contains the authentic word for those who would win a hearing for the eternal gospel from this unbelieving but desperately needy generation.

E. W. B.

CONTENTS

ix

PART ONE

INTRODUCTION

INTRODUCTION

WE are living in a world where, both in thought and in practice, a serious attempt is being made to keep religion and morality apart. Up to a point such a separation is feasible, at any rate in theory. Indeed, for clear thinking a distinction between the two is essential. Religion is concerned with a man's relation to God, morality with his relation to other people, and there are those who would maintain that religious and moral activities can remain independent of each other. The characteristic activities of the religious life are worship and prayer, those of the moral life right dealings with one's fellows which spring from such qualities as truthfulness and honesty. Frequently belief and behaviour march together and religious believers also display these moral qualities, but not invariably nor of necessity. Everyone, for example, is familiar with the gibe that some people who neither attend church nor appear to have any interest in religious truth live better lives than some professing Christians. This is a matter of common observation, but it proves nothing at all except the ability of those concerned in both camps to isolate these two spheres of human activity. Religion then becomes a cult, satisfying man's instinct for worship but involving him in no moral obligation in consequence. There have been many such cults in the history of religion, and, although we shall seek to show that such an attitude is a travesty of Christianity, it must be confessed that many sincere Christian believers appear unaware that faith should find its expression in practice. Conversely, it is by no means a rare phenomenon to discover conscientious men and women, as concerned about the good life as any Christian, who would at the same time emphatically deny that this concern is in any way bound up with, let alone dependent on, religious belief or practice.

Though I believe this view to be profoundly mistaken, it is no part of the object of this book to seek to refute it. Indeed, I have already attempted to do this in another place. Questions such as the existence and character of God, the nature of goodness, and the reasons why men should strive after it, while obviously related to this theme, are outside the scope of this inquiry. All that is written here assumes that God exists and that He has revealed His character and purpose supremely in Jesus Christ. On the basis of this assumption, its aim is to show that, whether or not there can be true morality apart from religion, the Christian religion in its fulness cannot be separated from the good life, not merely as an expression or consequence of Christian faith but as an essential element in the salvation which is offered to us in Jesus.

I would, however, in passing observe that, although many would maintain with undoubted sincerity that their interest in and devotion to the good life is entirely devoid of religious content, it

by no means follows that they are right in this dis-
claimer. Such people would probably describe
themselves as possessing conscientiousness without
religion, but others would regard that as a contra-
diction in terms. Conscience is an activity of a
man's whole personality pronouncing judgement
or giving guidance, and, while clearly there is a
human element in it, deriving from the environment in which it operates and the standards
current at the time and place, believers in God in
all ages have regarded conscience as the voice of
God speaking to men in their own hearts, albeit
mixed up with other elements from human
sources. It is this which gives conscience its
imperative quality, from which there is no appeal.
That is as true, for example, of the Greek drama-
tists in the fourth century before Christ, as of the
Christian believer in the twentieth century after
Him. Christians themselves would never claim
that what comes through the special channel of
Jesus Christ is all that men know of God. The very
fact that the moral agnostic or professed atheist
responds to the voice of conscience is in Christian
eyes an evidence of the gracious, though unrecog-
nized influence of the Spirit of God. Such men,
moreover, by the noble ideals they cherish and to
which they not seldom attain, are a constant rebuke
to some of us who profess more but all too often
attain less. This may well explain in part the
surprises which a study of the New Testament
leads us to suppose await us in heaven.

Our concern here, however, is not with the unbelieving moralist but with the Christian believer.

Whether or not there can be true morality without religion, the Christian religion by its very nature is concerned with morals. 'The storm centre of religious controversy,' wrote the late Dean Inge, 'in post-war Europe and America is, it seems to me, the relation of the gospel of Christ to problems of conduct. If the authority of Christ were rejected in this field, what would be left of Christianity would not be worth quarrelling over.'

It is at this point that we may best recognize the two factors which in recent years have tended to obscure this vital relationship of religion and morality in the minds of many theologians.

While recognizing the sincerity of those moralists who display conscientiousness and claim it has no religious basis or content, most Christians would profoundly disagree with them. In my country, where in the last generation religious observance and moral standards have alike steadily declined, Christians see a direct connection between these two phenomena. A dwindling Church is only too significant a sign of a perishing world. If religion is bowed out of the door, morality very soon disappears through the window. Behind every standard of conduct must be the ultimate standard of the will of God. Right is right, not because right actions make for the greatest happiness of all concerned, though this is true, but because the world and everything in it were created by God who is Himself all goodness, and men and women are His children. Conversely, wrong is wrong, not merely because it is socially inconvenient and brings suffering to ourselves and other people, though that is true, but because it is rebellion against God to whom we belong. When we are considering how men ought to behave and what kind of society they should seek to create, it is neither their physical mechanism nor their intellectual capacity that is the determining factor but the nature of men as children of God, made by Him and for Him, the objects of His continual care and redemptive activity.

Recognizing this truth, Christians, distressed at the progressive decline of moral standards, and concerned at the urgency of this matter, feel they must needs proclaim the Christian religion as the only firm foundation on which individual and social morality can rest, and by so doing are constantly running the risk that those whom they thus address, and even they themselves, will come to regard religion as the handmaid or sanction of morality. Sensitive to this danger and determined to avoid any such suggestion, they rightly insist that religion stands in its own right. God is God, and alone worthy to be adored by men and women whom He has made. All too often, however, in their anxiety not to put the cart before the horse, they allow the horse to canter away without the cart attached.

The other factor involved is the emphasis in much recent theological thought on the sovereignty of God and the helplessness of man. This no doubt is to a large degree a reaction against the easy-going liberalism of late nineteenth-century theology. But, as is almost inevitable in such matters, the pendulum has swung too far. Morality, in the

B

minds of these theologians, appears to be not only irrelevant but a positive danger to true evangelical religion. Humanism in any form is the deadly foe. As Professor Jessop has observed, 'Theology has been so engaged with the notion that morality is not enough as to have little taste for the semi-independent study of Christian morality.' The result has been a pessimistic view of human nature that would doubtless be justified if man could be considered apart from God, but that cannot be accepted if we take seriously the teaching of the Gospel that man can never properly be so considered. God seeks him and never abandons the quest, and there is in the worst of men that to which He can and does appeal. A study of the gospels themselves reveals that our Lord had far more faith in men than have many of our latter-day theologians. To quote Dr Jessop again, 'The contrast of divine holiness and human sinfulness must be present, yet can be so devastating as to take all joy out of religion.' Total despair of ourselves and total reliance on God for salvation is indeed a salutary and necessary attitude, but not if it is interpreted in such a way as to discourage all moral effort. 'By grace have ye been saved through faith, and that not of yourselves: it is the gift of God: not of works, that no man should glory.' To that we must cling, but we must also remember that a gift to be a blessing needs to be appropriated, and that what man cannot do on his own initiative can be brought about and can only be brought about by a response of a man's whole being to the forgiving and renewing grace of God. 'Work out your own salvation with fear and trembling; for it is God which worketh in you, both to will and to work.' The sovereignty of God is the sovereignty of love, and sovereign love seeks a reciprocal love. In the light of God's love, our view of human nature changes from unrelieved pessimism to joyous optimism.

Underlying all this misunderstanding there has been an inadequate appreciation of the content of salvation. Morality, we are told, is not the ground of our acceptance by God but the consequence of it. If by that we mean that any merit we may possess plays no part in our salvation, that is true. Stated in its simplest terms, the gospel is that what man can neither buy nor achieve, what he certainly can never deserve, is offered to him by God as a free gift. But what is this priceless gift? Wherein does it consist? Not, surely, in the formal cancelling of a debt we can never repay, though that may be incidentally involved, nor in the promise of a place in heaven rather than hell, for those are terms that need to be defined. The penalty of sin is not some arbitrary and fearful punishment that is visited upon us by an angry God, but consists rather in what we ourselves become as a consequence of the separation from God brought about by our sin. Salvation, therefore, concerns the kind of people we are, and the kind of people we are enabled to become by God's grace and through God's power. It begins here and now with the free forgiveness of our sins. There is nowhere else for it to begin. But forgiveness is no impersonal operation. Essentially it involves our relationship to God, which is restored as a result of His divine initiative and our human response. Because it is communion with God it is limitless. Henceforth a new principle is at work within man. Re-admission into fellowship with God is only the first of His gifts in salvation. There flows from that the continuous process whereby, through the operation of the Holy Spirit, the redeemed sinner, as Paul puts it, is gradually 'transformed into the same image from glory to glory'. Full salvation is the end of that process in time or eternity. This quite clearly involves at every stage a man's true being, his conduct and, more importantly, his character. Christian morality, then, is not so much a consequence of man's acceptance by God as one vital element in that gift of God we call salvation.

All Christians will agree that Jesus Christ is central in our religion. The Christian faith and the Christian Church alike are founded on the belief that nineteen centuries ago God became man. 'The Word was made flesh and dwelt among us and we beheld His glory.'

> *Our God contracted to a span,*
> *Incomprehensibly made Man.*

In Jesus the character and purpose of the eternal God were revealed as being what men would never have guessed them to be as a result of their reflection on their own experience or on the universe around them. In word and in deed Jesus revealed in time the character of the eternal God.

This revelation culminated in His redemptive death and His glorious resurrection. 'Having loved His own, He loved them to the end.' The Christian movement began because the first disciples responded to Him, and it has continued and spread whenever and wherever men and women who have heard the story of Jesus have made a similar response to Him as Lord and Saviour.

In the first century, however, the main expansion of the Church was due not to any of our Lord's first disciples but to Paul, the convert from Judaism, who from being an assiduous persecutor of the early Church became its outstanding apostle. It was he who both proclaimed the fact of what God had done in Jesus and became its first great interpreter. It was he who, with unerring instinct, steered the vessel which carried the infant Christian Church and its fortunes through a narrow channel full of rocks and shoals into the open sea, and was thus largely instrumental in making Christianity a world religion. His conversion meant for him an entirely new view of life's meaning. His fixed ideas were uprooted and he plunged into virgin forests of thought, as a result of which he laid foundations of Christian theology for all time so successfully that the late Dean Inge observed that 'there has been no religious revival within Christianity that has not been, on one side at least, a return to St Paul'. In consequence, his incidental correspondence has been 'Holy Scripture' for sixty generations of Christians. Of necessity, his task being what it was, his letters concentrate on those central doctrines of our

redemption which spring from our Lord's Passion
and resurrection. 'I determined not to know anything among you, save Jesus Christ, and him
crucified,' he wrote to the Corinthians, and later in
the same epistle, 'I delivered unto you first of all
that which also I received, how that Christ died
for our sins according to the Scriptures; and that
he was buried; and that he hath been raised on the
third day.' These were the redemptive acts in con-
seqence of which the Church had come into being,
and it was imperative that Christian preaching
should both proclaim them and interpret their
meaning. It is these same affirmations which find
their place in the historic creeds and form the
subject matter of the great majority of Christian
hymns, both ancient and modern.

But because this is so, and inevitably so, it
should not be assumed that either Paul or the
framers of the creeds were ignorant of or indifferent to the earlier ministry and teaching of our
Lord. Though Paul's writings are earlier than any
of the gospels in their present form, stories of Jesus
and accounts of His teaching were already current
among Christians, and, quite obviously, the gospels included in the canon of Scripture were
familiar to the early fathers. Neither Paul nor the
fathers thought of Jesus as someone unknown
until the events of the Passion, and it is a great
mistake to contrast the Jesus of the gospels and the
Christ of the epistles as if they were different
persons. The Cross is indeed central in the Christian faith, 'towering o'er the wrecks of time', but it
is not isolated. Jesus is the same yesterday, today

and for ever. The hands and feet that were nailed to the Cross were the hands that had washed the disciples' feet, and the feet that had trod the streets and lanes of Galilee on errands of mercy. The whole point of the passion story is that it was Jesus who died and rose again, He who spake as no man ever spake, and lived a life of unequalled purity and love, and who, when all that gracious words and loving deeds could do was of no avail, rather than abandon His mission of redemption, gave Himself utterly for sinful men and women.

In the light of this, the Saviourhood and the teaching of our Lord should surely be regarded as belonging to each other. Paul was not primarily a moral reformer. His immediate concern was to preach Jesus and the resurrection, but he was quick to suspect the genuineness of any response to that teaching that did not manifest itself in character and conduct. Though his extant writings make no reference to the ministry and teaching of our Lord, he composed the incomparable 'Hymn of Love', which has been aptly described as Paul's biography of Jesus, and which would certainly never have been written except with our Lord in mind.

The inseparable relationship between Christian faith and morals is even more clearly demonstrated when we consider our Lord Himself. His earliest disciples did not indeed come to regard Him as divine as a result of their reflection on His moral excellence; it was rather the direct impression made on them by His whole personality which led them to this belief. But they very soon came to recognize His moral perfection, so that the writer to the Hebrews does not hesitate to speak of Him as 'tempted in all points even as we are, yet without sin'. And there can be no doubt that if their contemplation of His character had led them to any other conclusion, their belief in His divinity would soon have waned. Nor should we ignore our Lord's oft-repeated insistence in this matter: 'Not every one that saith unto me, Lord, Lord, shall enter into the Kingdom of Heaven, but he that doeth the will of my Father'; and again: 'By their fruits ye shall know them', implying not that it is works rather than faith which find acceptance with God, but that fruits or their absence are the undeniable evidence of the reality of a man's faith or lack of it.

No characteristic of the contemporary scene is more disturbing than the apparent failure of many evangelistic enterprises. Somehow or other, though the Church recognizes its primary responsibility in this matter, and certainly does not relax its efforts, it seems to be unable to win a response to the proclamation of the gospel on any scale commensurate with those efforts. Even when sincere and earnest evangelists meet with some immediate success, it often proves shortlived. Genuine as the spiritual experience of the convert may have been at the time, it does not develop into permanent Christian discipleship.

Rightly or wrongly, it is the conviction of the present writer that this is largely due to the changed conditions of life today in which the gospel must needs be proclaimed. In the days of the evangelical revival, for example, the masses of people were predominantly concerned with their own lot in their immediate surroundings. There was at best only a vague awareness of what was happening in the wider world. In such circumstances many heard the gospel and responded to it as it affected their own present condition and eternal welfare, without either the opportunity or the desire to relate it to world events or theories of the meaning of history.

Today, however, man knows himself to be a citizen of the world. He is alike fascinated and frightened by the vast new resources at his disposal, the misuse of which may issue in ultimate disaster for civilization itself. He lives in a society where, though more is known about the origin of man, less seems certain about his destiny. He shares the general doubts concerning the true nature of man, and in consequence is uncertain what kind of person he ought to be and what kind of society he should be striving to create. It is often said that he lacks a sense of sin, but this is a superficial judgement. Very few men, if pressed to analyse their own character and conduct, would hesitate to admit their own sinfulness, though they might not use that word. It is rather that his sense of personal sin is bound up with a sense that he belongs to a world that has gone wrong. It leaps out at him from newspaper headlines and television programmes. This is the situation which commands his attention and dominates his thoughts. In relation to this, the 'plan of salvation', as set forth by Paul and persisting in our evangelical proclamation, often seems remote, as though not belonging to the real world in which men are absorbed whether they so will or not. There is a gulf between the thought-world in which the facts concerning our redemption are proclaimed and the thought-world inhabited by contemporary men and women for most of their time. The need today is not for the proclamation of the gospel on a larger scale to people who have never heard it (though that need doubtless still exists in some regions as yet untouched by missionary enterprise); the main task is to interpret to men in the situation in which they find themselves what they have already heard but have failed to understand or relate to their present condition.

Evangelism, to be effective in the present situation, demands not so much the proclamation of the message as the education or re-education of those to whom it has been proclaimed in the past. Men need to be brought to an awareness of reality and a true understanding of what man really is. This is a much more difficult and formidable task than dealing with mass assemblies. It is a task only successfully to be performed with individuals in groups, and it is significant that the most hopeful signs in Church life are to be seen where group activity is practised. In other words, the evangelism which is needed is a teaching evangelism, and the Church needs to be recalled to a teaching ministry. This teaching ministry must be based on the teaching of Jesus, which will be found to provide the essential bridge between the great doctrines of our salvation and the realities of everyday life in the world where that salvation can become an effective and transforming influence.

It is necessary to bear constantly in mind what we have and what we have not in the teaching of Jesus as it has come down to us. It contains no comprehensive code of behaviour to which we can refer when in doubt as to the course of action to be rightly pursued. Indeed, there are many occasions when it is of little use to ask in a particular situation, 'What would Jesus do?' Most of us would not be capable of the feat of imagination required to visualize Jesus in the given situation, the superficial conditions of life being so different today from those obtaining nineteen centuries ago. Indeed, it is safe to say that, had our Lord attempted that kind of detailed instruction, His teaching would have become obsolete long ago. It is more profitable to realize that in every situation there is a will of God for us, and to inquire, 'What would God have me to do?' The surest way of discovering the answer to that question is to turn to the teaching of our Lord and ponder it, seeking at the same time the guidance of the Holy Spirit that we may interpret it correctly. For what we have in the teaching of Jesus is an insight into reality which never becomes obsolete, a temper of mind independent alike of the ravages of time and changing circumstances, because it reveals the mind of the eternal God.

This does not mean that the teaching of our Lord was couched in vague generalities; on the contrary, when, as in the Sermon on the Mount, He enunciated abstract moral principles, they were clear and unmistakable. Furthermore, those same principles were illuminated in His incomparable parables, where concrete images drawn from every-day life became the vehicles of eternal truth.

More importantly even than this, the teaching of Jesus found its perfect embodiment in Himself. To contemplate His teaching is to be brought face to face with the Teacher. Had this not been so, it may be questioned whether, in spite of its sub-limity, His teaching would still be challenging men and nations. It might well ere this have been dismissed as impracticable idealism, out of touch with reality, as indeed many do seek to dismiss it. That such attempts are doomed to failure is due to our Lord Himself, who invested it with eternal significance. Others have said, 'Love one another'; only He could say, 'Love one another even as I have loved you.' Having taught that the real test of character is how a man behaves towards those who hate and misuse him, our Lord was put to the test of His own standards, and the gracious words spoken on the Galilean hillside found their glorious echo on the hill of Calvary: 'Father, forgive them, for they know not what they do.' In parable after parable He described the true nature of the King-dom of God, but He Himself remains the supreme parable. In Him the Kingdom had come, the rule of God was demonstrated, meeting and conquering every earthly power; and the inescapable question every man must face is, 'What think ye of Christ?'

'Heaven and earth shall pass away, but my words shall not pass away', Jesus is reported as claiming. The ground of this claim is that in word, as in

deed, our Lord revealed the Father. Characteristic-
ally, when enjoining some attitude or course of
action, the reason He adduced was 'that ye may be
sons of your Father which is in heaven', and the
command or promise which sums up His teaching,
'Be ye perfect' or 'Ye shall be perfect', is followed
by the same unequivocal explanation 'even as your
Father in heaven is perfect'. This understanding
of the Father's will and undeviating loyalty to it is
the key to all that our Lord said and did, and it
could be said that Christianity stands or falls by
the validity of our Lord's spiritual consciousness
and insight. If He was mistaken, then His life and
character remain a glorious episode in human
history, silhouetted against a background of mean-
ingless nonsense. If, however, as Christians believe, He was right, then in His words and deeds, in
Himself, is Reality. The redemption He wrought is
valid in time and in eternity, and those who respond to His love can themselves be re-made into
His likeness and receive power to re-make the
world, for it is His world, and His rule alone can
bring happiness and blessing to mankind.

If this be true, the teaching of Jesus is immediately seen to be of paramount importance. It is not
just a consequence or working out of the gospel; it
is part of the gospel itself. Proclamation of the
good news and teaching about the good life are as
inseparable as two sides of a penny. A man who
responds to the redemptive love of God in Jesus is
saved from his sins, but not into a vacuum. He is
now in a new relationship to God, living in God's
kingdom, according to God's rule. The Saviour,

as a continuing part of His saving activity, becomes a Teacher, illumining the mind of the converted disciple, communicating His own insight into reality, empowering him that the kingdom of God, the gracious rule of God, may have free course in him. Through that teaching he comes to know his Saviour better, every part of his life takes on a new significance, and as he responds he receives power to bear his witness and play his part in a world which is perishing, but which is God's world, which He made and loves, which He seeks to save but can only save as the men and women in it also turn from their sins and accept His Lordship and live in His Kingdom.

PART TWO

EXPOSITION

'BLESSED'

IN the light of the foregoing considerations, let us proceed to an examination of the teaching of our Lord, taking as a basis His sketch of the ideal character contained in the Beatitudes, recorded in the first gospel. For this purpose we can afford to ignore critical questions, such as the relationship of the two versions found in Matthew and Luke respectively. Such matters, interesting and important as they may be to New Testament scholars, are outside the scope of this inquiry. Suffice it to say that, although it is frequently assumed that the more primitive form in Luke is more likely to be original, this is by no means established, and the late Dr Oman, for example, makes out a strong case the other way. We need to bear in mind that only a comparatively small proportion has been preserved of what must have been a considerable body of teaching, and no one suggests that there has been any significant distortion in the summary contained in the Sermon on the Mount. It is quite probable that at different times Jesus uttered both forms. Anyway there the teaching is, and there it would remain even though the wildest attacks on the historicity of the gospel narrative were substantiated, which is far from being the case. Let us suppose, for example, that the fantastic contention, once put forward but utterly discredited, that Jesus of Nazareth never lived proved to be valid; we should still be faced with the Beatitudes, and behind the teaching a teacher.

Moreover, the Beatitudes, though they may be considered as a compact whole in themselves, can repeatedly be illustrated from and illuminated by the parables, as we shall seek to show. This serves to emphasize what is here our particular concern, namely that in essence the Beatitudes are religious, and to regard them as merely a collection of moral precepts or a set of rules to be observed is to miss their real significance. The parables are explicitly parables of the Kingdom of God, and no one, whatever his judgement upon them, would question their religious character. Similarly, the Beatitudes, though cast in the form of comment upon moral qualities, are revealed as religious if in no other way than by the consequences which attend the possession of these qualities and ratify them as authentic. The poor in spirit, for example, possess the Kingdom of Heaven, the pure in heart see God, and the peacemakers shall be called sons of God. The state of being portrayed in the Beatitudes is to be attained not by effort but by insight, or perhaps, we should say, by the spontaneous effort which follows upon insight. To become like this is to be saved, and salvation can neither be earned nor achieved but must be accepted as the gift of God.

Furthermore, in contemplating parables and beatitudes alike, we are brought face to face with the Teacher, for Jesus Himself is the perfect embodiment of His teaching; and in this encounter there is revealed to us the one sure clue to the character of the eternal God, for not only did our

Lord reveal that character in all He was and did, but He also made it the sanction for the rule of life He enjoined upon men. The Beatitudes, therefore, are both religious and theological. 'Looking at God through the Beatitudes' might well be a description of the exercise upon which we are engaged. This is not to ignore the moral nature of this teaching, but to confirm, if confirmation were needed, that in the Christian faith religion and morals are indissolubly joined.

'He opened His mouth and taught them saying "Blessed . . .".' It must be admitted that the word 'blessed' presents an initial difficulty for the ordinary reader. With the lapse of time the word has acquired a sanctimonious flavour, conveying an entirely erroneous impression. Indeed, it has almost become a technical term. In endeavouring to avoid this, some modern translators use the word 'happy'. This does, indeed, overcome the particular difficulty, but it is doubtful if it does justice to the full meaning of the word, unless we always remember that it is happiness of a very special quality that is denoted. The only really satisfactory solution would be to rescue the word 'blessed' and restore its original richness of content. The *New English Bible* attempts this with some success by investing the sayings with a natural spontaneity; 'How blest are those . . .' Whatever word we use, it should be one which will appeal to the ordinary man as a description of a state of being eminently to be desired. From this point of view, the word 'happy' has much to commend it. It will be recalled that not very long ago there was a popular song with the haunting refrain, 'I want to be happy', which was on everybody's lips. How often it occurs that a song wins and retains its popularity because its superficial gaiety conceals a sound and deep religious instinct. Millions who would never have dreamed of singing, 'Through the night of doubt and sorrow', or 'Lead us, Heavenly Father, lead us', marched to the strains of 'It's a long long way to Tipperary' and 'There's a long long trail a-winding', both of which express in their own idiom the pilgrim idea. Many were helped to a spiritual triumph over adversity by 'Pack up your troubles in your old kitbag', thereby revealing a genuine, if imperfectly articulate, religious aspiration and feeling. So it was with 'I want to be happy'. Happiness is a natural, human and reasonable aim. However long it eludes us, it ever remains a fascinating possibility. Even if we are not happy, deep down we feel we ought to be. In the contemporary world there is a prevailing pessimism which reflects the disillusion amounting to despair which has settled like a blight on man's hopes concerning himself and the world. Books and plays expressing a deep-seated cynicism abound. The authors would justify them as being 'realist'. Happy endings, on the other hand, are often dismissed contemptuously as bad art. But the function of art is to express the beautiful and the true. Those who depict reality as sordid and ugly, sincere and accomplished as they often are, perform a grave disservice to their fellows, against which the deepest instincts of our being rise in revolt. It is too bad to be true.

Against this philosophy of hopelessness stands the gospel, and behind the gospel the Teacher Himself, who says, 'Blessed . . .'

Jesus was a realist. His message to men was positive. A generation ago a New Testament scholar caused a stir by stating that Jesus did not denounce sin. The remark was not strictly true, for He certainly denounced the sins of the Pharisees, but that was because the only hope for them was to be startled out of their complacency. The bulk of men and women He viewed with compassion, as He saw them like sheep without a shepherd, missing the happiness they were meant to enjoy. John the Baptist had come with denunciations, summoning men to repentance, and that was the limit of his power. If our Lord neither denounced nor despised, it was because He could help. Denunciation then becomes not only unnecessary but a hindrance. It hurt Him to see men missing that 'blessedness' He proclaimed, and in His teaching He told them how to find it. Happiness, if we take the Beatitudes as our guide, is not a thing to be directly sought. Indeed, that is the sure way to miss it. It is rather a by-product or accompaniment of a certain state of being. In this it differs profoundly from pleasure, which is derived from the satisfaction of some appetite, and by its very nature is temporary and passes, though, of course, it may be repeated. This, said Jesus, is the sort of person one can congratulate a man upon being, poor in spirit, a mourner, and so on. Analysing the Beatitudes more closely, we see they are all concerned with right relationships, and here again is a field where religion and morality both belong. The moralist recognizes that right behaviour involves a man's relationship with other people. Our lives are so bound up with each other that it must be so. The moralist recognizes also that man is a complex being and needs to come to terms with himself. He is several selves rolled into one, and needs what psychologists call 'integration'. The religious man recognizes the importance of these two categories of relationship, but adds a third. Man's primary need is right relationship to God, which is not independent of his other relationships but is bound up with them. A man cannot be in a right relationship to God while his relationship with his fellow men is wrong, and his relationship to God and his fellow men will inevitably be confused unless he has achieved unity within his own personality.

So nine times in solemn iteration our Lord draws attention to some facet of the character of a man who can really be called happy. All these, it should be noted, are facets of the same ideal character. Our Lord did not give a catalogue of nine different kinds of people, all of whom are blest. Together these qualities in perfect balance constitute what God intends man to become, what any man may become who goes to school with Jesus, learns of Him, and submits himself to His saving grace.

In recent years many bookshelves have contained mammoth volumes entitled *Mathematics for the million* and *Science for the million*, vast compendia of information compiled for the benefit of those of us who are deficient in these fields of knowledge. In much briefer compass the Beatitudes set forth the way to 'Happiness for the million'. They are for ordinary men and women such as we are in this very world we live in. We do not need to explore unimagined vistas, or seek specialized experiences. We neither need to escape from self, seeking the way of the Buddhists, nor to set our teeth in defiance, following that of the Stoics. The hero of the Beatitudes shirks no duty and shuns no sorrow, but finds in the varied experiences of life the raw material of that happiness which underlies all experience, if he has the qualities the Beatitudes describe.

Our Lord Himself was a supremely happy man. He was a Man of Sorrows, acquainted with grief, but happiness and sorrow are not inconsistent with each other. If He had evaded the sorrow that was inseparable from the fulfilment of His mission, He would have forfeited His happiness. It was 'for the joy that was set before Him' that He endured the Cross, despising the shame. Because He saw the world as God's world, men and women as God's children, and Himself as the instrument of the Father's will of love, He was enabled to meet every challenge and win a spiritual victory over all the evil things in life and over death itself, and with a victor's authority He beckons us to learn of Him and then to follow Him, and so to find through Him our happiness.

THE POOR IN SPIRIT

D R OMAN described this first Beatitude as
'the keynote which determines the religious
music of the whole'. Certainly, if once we grasp
the truth it contains, the subsequent ones follow
naturally, whereas if we fail to grasp its truth, the
others are likely to remain inexplicable paradoxes.

The Beatitude itself presents us with an initial
difficulty. Who in fact are the poor in spirit?
Obviously neither the poor-spirited nor the spiritually poor answer to the description. The *New
English Bible* seems to me to draw out the true
meaning admirably with the rendering, 'How blest
are those who know that they are poor.' The whole
teaching of our Lord concerning riches and
poverty affords a valuable clue to the interpretation
of this Beatitude. 'Blessed are ye poor', He is
reported by Luke as saying, and this is consistent
with the well-known passages which stress the
dangers inseparable from riches. It is not that
poverty itself is a blessing. It is often a curse, and
it may be the direct consequence of wickedness or
laziness. Nor are riches themselves inevitably a
curse. If they were, it is hardly conceivable that
the rich young ruler would have been encouraged
to bestow his wealth on others. A rich man may be
poor in spirit. It is a delightful experience to meet
such a man, partially perhaps because it contains
an element of surprise. But the fact remains that a

rich man is less likely than a poor man to possess that consciousness of need which poverty of spirit implies. Riches bring a sense of independence which tends to obscure the sense of need and is therefore spiritually dangerous. In not a few spheres the idea of independence in recent times has exercised a quite disastrous fascination. Nations striving after independence have equated it with Utopia, only to find in the event that it has brought with it insoluble problems and responsibilities too great to bear. Our civilization itself, possessed of resources undreamed of by our grandfathers, and intoxicated by material wealth and new-found mastery in the scientific realm, is under the condemnation pronounced of old on the Church at Laodicea, 'You say "How rich I am! And how well I have done! I have everything I want in the world!" In fact, though you do not know it, you are the most pitiful wretch, poor, blind and naked.'

The problems of civilization are always the problems of the individual writ large, and the one hope for men and women and for the world is in that poverty of spirit which springs from a recognition of need. The gospel of Jesus is good news for men conscious of their need, healing for those who know they are sick, salvation for those who know they are in jeopardy. Material poverty is something of which we are inevitably aware. We may conceal it from others, though there is little incentive so to do, but we cannot conceal it from ourselves. We are constantly reminded of it in a thousand ways, nor is it anything to be ashamed of.

Spiritual poverty, on the other hand, most of us are loth to admit; and it is dangerously easy to conceal it not only from others but from ourselves. Typical examples are to be found in the parable of the Pharisee and the Publican and the parable of the Prodigal Son. Neither the Pharisee in the former parable nor the elder brother in the latter was a hypocrite in the accepted sense of a bad man pretending to be good. By all recognized standards they compared favourably with the Publican and the younger son. The trouble was that the spiritual pride induced by their relative excellence had banished any sense of need, so that the Pharisee's prayer could not be heard and the elder brother could not bring himself, in spite of his father's importunity, to enter the house and sit at table with his scapegrace brother. Truly 'God resisteth the proud, but giveth grace to the humble'. In the last analysis, sin is always human pride setting itself against God. This is true in every sphere. Blessed are they who know that they are ignorant, not because ignorance is a blessing but because awareness of ignorance is the gateway to knowledge. The cocksure, who think they know everything, have ceased to be teachable. So God draws nigh to the poor and needy, and, if we have not found Him, it is because we have not wanted to do so desperately enough. As Mary sang in the Magnificat, 'The arrogant of heart and mind He has put to rout, He has torn imperial powers from their thrones, but the humble have been lifted high, the hungry He has satisfied with good things, the rich sent empty away.'

Those who realize their poverty and are conscious of their spiritual need find their blessing in complete dependence upon God. They have discovered that independence is a chimera. This is universally true. The richest man in the world is dependent at every point on his fellows. He depends on them for recognition of the validity of his wealth, whatever form it takes. He depends on their willingness to fetch and carry for him, to manufacture and make available the countless things he needs. If independence of our fellow men is a vain boast, the claim to independence of God borders on lunacy. It is He who gives us life and strength and all things. The poor in spirit not only recognize this, but realize that it is man's glory not his shame; by putting their trust in God, and God alone, they discover God to be entirely dependable, and the whole range of experience to be within His providential control. The man who glories in his independence and regards the world as an appropriate scene for the satisfaction of his own desires and purposes must select experiences and seek to manipulate events to that end, and sooner or later the world will overcome him. The poor in spirit, who see the world as God's world and themselves as His children, discover all experience to be raw material which can be woven into the fabric of a blessed life. The Kingdom of Heaven is theirs, and the blessing they receive knows no limits; for, living under the rule of God, they are always making fresh discoveries and embarking on new adventures in response to the promptings of God's Spirit, just as the humble seeker after knowledge is always discovering that the more he comes to know, the more remains yet to be known. So the poor in spirit grow continually in grace, whereas the tragedy of the proud is that, their spiritual horizon being bounded by their own vision, and their attainments limited by their own unaided efforts, they remain unaware of their own possibilities and never become the people their Maker intends them to be.

This poverty of spirit finds expression in the familiar words of the Methodist Covenant Service: 'I am no longer my own, but Thine. Put me to what Thou wilt, rank me with whom Thou wilt; put me to doing, put me to suffering; let me be employed for Thee or laid aside for Thee, exalted for Thee or brought low for Thee; let me be full, let me be empty; let me have all things, let me have nothing; I freely and heartily yield all things to Thy pleasure and disposal.'

Such poverty of spirit runs counter to the maxims which normally find favour among men and determine their attitude to life. We have seen already that, regarded merely as a principle governing human relationships and activities, as, for example, the search for knowledge, it is demonstrably valid. In what has been said, however, we have not hesitated to relate it to man's religious attitude, and in particular his relationship to God. We are justified in doing this not only by the religious consequence attached to the Beatitude (theirs is the Kingdom of Heaven), but also by the fact that it is quite impossible to consider this saying apart from the life and character of Jesus

Himself. It brings us immediately face to face with the staggering paradox at the heart of the Christian religion. 'Ye know', wrote Paul, 'the grace of our Lord Jesus Christ, that, though He was rich, yet for your sakes He became poor, that ye through His poverty might become rich.' Nothing about Jesus is more wonderful than His great humility. 'Being in the form of God, He counted it not a prize to be on an equality with God, but emptied Himself, taking the form of a servant, being made in the likeness of men; and, being found in fashion as a man, He humbled Himself.' As He entered this world by a lowly door, so He lived. His was no sheltered life; He possessed no wealth, no worldly position. He enjoyed no lasting popularity, nor any favour of the great. The loyalty of His friends failed, and even at one point, it would seem, the divine consolation. Shame, defeat, agony and death were His lot. But by the spiritual triumph He won over these dread antagonists, He displayed how these evil things could reveal the glory of God, and in Him supremely the Kingdom of Heaven was revealed. The secret of it all was His utter dependence on His Father and obedience to Him. 'I can of myself do nothing', He declared.

But even this is not the deepest truth. That is to be found earlier in the same discourse, where our Lord is reported as saying, 'The son can do nothing of himself, but what he seeth the father doing: for what things soever he doeth, these the son also doeth in like manner.' This saying would have been beyond the wildest religious imagination to invent, and it is only as we contemplate our Lord that we can even begin to understand and then adore. In His humility our Lord was not doing something of Himself, but what He saw the Father doing. John here consistently sees further into the mystery than Paul in the passage quoted above. So he recounts that, 'Jesus, knowing that the Father had given all things into his hands, and that he came forth from God, and goeth to God', in the consciousness, that is, of His divine origin and destiny, 'riseth from supper . . . and took a towel.' So this first Beatitude points directly to this revolutionary idea of God on which the Christian religion rests, so contrary to all that man's natural imagination would suggest, and indeed all other religions declare. The one eternal God, Maker and Sustainer of the universe, came to man in great humility. It is in the light of that amazing but glorious truth that we receive His word, 'Blessed are the poor in spirit: for theirs is the Kingdom of Heaven.'

THE MOURNERS

LIKE the first Beatitude, this too runs counter to a favourite maxim of the world which regards sorrow as an experience to be shunned as far as possible. Yet Jesus, the Author of the religion of joy, pronounces a benediction upon sorrow. One reason for the strangeness with which this falls upon our ears may well be due to the traditional trappings of mourning which are no longer acceptable in our present-day society. Indeed, the use of the very word almost inevitably conjures up the vision of a funeral cortège, but, if we are to understand this saying, we must recognize that the word is used here in a much wider sense, and involves mourning for the living even more than for the dead.

Perhaps the quickest way to appreciate the significance of mourning is to try to imagine what a refusal ever to mourn would imply. Sorrow and sadness may be unwelcome visitors, but inability or unwillingness to admit them into our experience, even if that were possible, would involve isolating ourselves from our fellows and, as we shall later see, from God Himself. It would involve the loss of all the good things that fellowship brings. In the real world, we are capable of sorrow because we care. Only if we did not care would it be possible to avoid all grief. 'Foolishly,' wrote Francis Thompson, 'we shun this shunless sadness; fondly we deem of her as but huntress of men, who is tender and the bringer of tenderness to those she visits with her fearful favours. A world without joy were more tolerable than a world without sorrow. Without sadness, where were brotherliness?'

Furthermore, mourning is an inescapable accompaniment to that poverty of spirit we have already examined. As we have seen, the poor in spirit neither desire nor need to manipulate events for their own satisfaction, but rely upon the divine resources to meet every experience of life. Such an attitude, however, of necessity involves them in facing the hard realities of the world as it is; not only the suffering inseparable from the chances and changes of this mortal life, as these affect themselves and their loved ones, but the vast volume of distress which results from war and lesser forms of social evil. The mourner who cares cannot for one moment be indifferent to these things on the physical and material plane, and, being spiritually sensitive, will agonize even more over the human sinfulness of which they are a consequence. Such active mourning will guard against the danger which otherwise attends poverty of spirit – that acceptance of life's discipline may degenerate into passive resignation or even fatalism. 'I have learned,' wrote Paul, 'in whatsoever state I am, therein to be content.' The passage from the Methodist Covenant Service already quoted is an expansion of this.

Such readiness to accept without resentment the circumstances, however unideal, in which we find ourselves placed, is an essential element in blessed-ness as expounded by our Lord. But equally it must be recognized that such situations will usually present us with a challenge. Side by side with that contentment with our lot must be a divine discontent with everything that is evil in ourselves and in the world. Such divine discontent is characteristic of every spiritually healthy man and woman, and of every virile society. It must be distinguished from the petulant and fractious discontent of the children in the market-place, who, in our Lord's parable, always wanted to play at funerals when the others were playing at weddings, and vice versa. The divine discontent of the mourner is what makes him sensitive to evil, recognizing its presence but at the same time striving to overcome it. Nor in a Christian context is the overcoming of evil the final goal. The mourner realizes that even the good is the enemy of the best, and nothing short of perfection will satisfy him; for perfection is God's will for His children and His offer to them. We can observe and admire the spirit in the scientist whose every discovery leads him to fresh endeavour. Similarly, the true artist mourns because his best picture has yet to be painted, and the preacher because his best sermon is yet to be preached.

It was not the Israelites, who adapted themselves to the conditions in Babylon and, accepting their captivity, were gradually absorbed into its pagan society, whom God could use, but the mourning remnant who nursed the vision of a restored Jerusalem, and were ready to endure the rigours of the return journey and the task of rebuilding the windswept ruins. In like manner, to those who have glimpsed the vision of the Kingdom of Heaven, the evil conditions of earth, though widely tolerated, must be intolerable. Even less can any man who has begun to take Jesus seriously and measure himself by the standard of His teaching and character retain any shred of complacency about himself.

True mourning, moreover, is a sign of hope. We mourn because of what might have been: I might have been such a much better man; the world might have been such a much better place. Otherwise mourning is irrational and pointless. But at the same time we mourn for what can still be. If what we mourn over was not inevitable, neither need it be permanent. Neither we ourselves nor the world itself are finished products; the process of transformation can begin. The mourner is a realist, but also he must needs be an optimist with his face turned to the light – not indeed an optimist about unaided human nature, but an optimist who believes in the power of God to redeem fallen men and women and remake the world, which is His world, according to the pattern of His eternal Kingdom. Such mourners are themselves redeemed, and by allying themselves with the redemptive purpose of God's holy will, become His instruments of redemption even to the extent, in Paul's daring word, of filling up 'that which is lacking of the afflictions of Christ'. This is the mourning which is blessed, for it springs from faith in the triumph of God's holy love, which is comfort indeed.

Thus we are led to appreciate the essentially religious content of this second Beatitude, which, like the first, is rooted in our Lord's revelation of the character of God.

He who is never recorded as mourning for Himself took upon Himself the sorrows and afflictions of others. Well does Isaac Watts declare of Him,

> *Touched with a sympathy within,*
> *He knows our feeble frame.*

Quite early in Christ's ministry we are told that 'He saw a great multitude and he had compassion on them, because they were as sheep not having a shepherd'. Again and again in the healing miracles in the Synoptic gospels, in the encounters with Nicodemus and the woman of Samaria in the fourth gospel, and in the matchless story of the woman taken in adultery, this active sympathy of our Lord shines forth. He mourned for what might have been, and on one occasion wept over Jerusalem, as He contemplated the contrast between God's purpose for His people and their present plight. Supremely, when He hung on the Cross, enduring physical agony we can only dimly imagine, His thoughts and prayers were centred on those who had brought this about, whose dire need of help was so much greater than His own. So the religion of Jesus invites us to see the meaning of the world in the undeserved but redemptive agony of a good man. It was because He thus mourned that there was for Him no escape from the Cross.

He loved men too deeply either to abandon them or to compromise with them.

In this it was the Father's attitude He revealed and the Father's will to which He was obedient, 'for it became him, for whom are all things and through whom are all things, in bringing many sons unto glory, to make the Author of their salvation perfect through sufferings.' By being the perfect Son, He revealed the perfect Father, who cares for His children with a divine love so amazing and at the same time so inexorable that He sent His Son to win them back to Himself and, when there was no other way, to die that they might be forgiven.

But He died not only 'that we might be forgiven' but also 'to make us good', and contemplation of the Cross of Jesus should disabuse our minds for ever of the immoral and unscriptural conception of salvation as merely some formal cancellation of debt or remission of penalty. The Saviour who died for men is the Saviour who mourned for their sins, and the Father who sent Him is the Father who made us for Himself, and who cares too deeply ever to be indifferent to the kind of people we are. It is this realization that the eternal God cares about us and mourns over us that evokes from us a glad response, whereby we accept the forgiveness which is ours through Jesus, and, wonder of wonders, receive power to enter into the fellowship of His sufferings and share in His redemptive purpose for the world.

'Blessed are they that mourn: for they shall be comforted.'

THE MEEK

THIS is the third and last of the first group of the Beatitudes, each of which runs counter to some generally accepted maxim. In one way it is the greatest paradox of them all, because of the astonishing consequence attached to it.

The man of the world who seeks material ends may look askance at the poor in spirit and the mourner, but he would be honest enough to admit his unfamiliarity with the Kingdom of Heaven and his lack of experience of the divine comfort which are stated to be the rewards of those virtues. He would lay no claim to these, which he would agree that God, if indeed there be a God, may indeed have at His disposal. But in allocating the earth to the meek Jesus is invading the world's territory, and seems guilty of a presumption which the facts neither support nor justify. We have only to look around, it would be said, to be seized of the absurdity of this proposition. The earth is a sphere where might is right, where the race is to the swift and the battle to the strong. The operative principle is the survival of the fittest and the devil take the hindmost. The meek man stands no chance at all in the frantic struggle for the prizes of earth.

What are we to say to these things? First of all, we need to correct the misconceptions of meekness which are popularly held. By doing this we shall not resolve the paradox, but it will be a different paradox. For there is no word in the language which in the course of time has come to acquire such erroneous associations in the popular mind. Doubtless Charles Wesley's children's hymn, 'Gentle Jesus, meek and mild', is partly responsible. Generations of children have learned this at their mother's knee, and in consequence meekness has become for them synonymous with mildness, whereas a little reflection would have served to show that the two must be different or the writer would not have indulged in a pointless repetition. As a corrective it is illuminating to consider a verse from another of Charles Wesley's hymns:

> *Jesus's tremendous name*
> *Puts all our foes to flight:*
> *Jesus, the meek, the angry Lamb,*
> *A Lion is in fight.*
> *By all hell's host withstood,*
> *We all hell's host o'erthrow:*
> *And conquering them, through Jesu's*
> *blood,*
> *We still to conquer go.*

Even so, the misconception of the meaning of the word is so deep-rooted and universally prevalent that it is unlikely ever to regain its proper significance in common speech. It is essential to our present purpose, however, if we are to understand this saying, that we should seek to redeem it from the erroneous associations which have gathered around it. Dr Oman defined true meekness as 'the relation to the Father of our spirits which, by laying us open to His whole purpose, shows us all things in the earth working for it'. If we accept that definition, it becomes clear that meekness is consistent with both poverty of spirit and the divine discontent which characterizes the mourner, while providing adequate safeguards against the dangers to which those virtues expose us. When, for example, opposition and disappointment are encountered, the meek man, having discerned the purpose of God underlying all that happens or ever can happen, neither allows his poverty of spirit to degenerate into resignation or despair, nor his divine discontent so to dominate him as to cause him to lose his patience and his temper. Such failure to achieve mastery over self inevitably results in the betrayal of the most worthy cause. But the meek man neither submits to evil nor compromises with it, but by active, persistent patience overcomes it. His demeanour, freed from inner tension, remains debonair throughout. This attitude of being had received classic exposition in the thirty-seventh Psalm, which doubtless was in our Lord's mind when He included this virtue in His picture of the blessed man. 'Fret not thyself because of evil doers, neither be thou envious against them that work unrighteousness . . . Rest in the Lord, and wait patiently for him: fret not thyself because of him who prospereth in his way, because of the man who bringeth wicked devices to pass. Cease from anger and forsake wrath: fret not thyself, it tendeth only to evil doing. For evil doers shall be cut off: but those that wait upon the Lord, they shall inherit the land. For yet a little while and the wicked shall not be . . . but the meek shall inherit the land.'

There can be no doubt that our Lord, who was well versed in the Scriptures, had this passage in mind and set His seal on it in this Beatitude.

When we appreciate that this virtue springs from and reveals an attitude to God and to the world as God's world, we understand the significance of the word 'inherit'. The man who puts his trust in material force and external sanctions may seize and hold vast tracts of the earth, but he will never inherit it. The man, on the other hand, who has glimpsed the Father's patient purpose, and, with undying faith in the character of God and loyalty to His methods, allies himself with it, may never own one square yard of it, but nevertheless as a son of the Father he enters upon it as his rightful inheritance which no person and no circumstance can wrench from him.

In another realm such an attitude may be observed in the scientist who, with an ineradicable faith in the intelligibility of things, pursues his patient investigations, undeterred by setbacks, until finally his research leads him to the discovery of some new truth, and he not only enters his kingdom of knowledge but also leads others into it.

Rudyard Kipling is hardly the writer to whom one most naturally turns for an exposition of the great Christian virtues, but he seems to display a genuine insight into the nature of true meekness in the poem which enjoyed a great vogue a generation ago:

If you can talk with crowds and keep your virtue,
* Or walk with kings, nor lose the common touch,*
If neither foes nor loving friends can hurt you,
* If all men count with you, but none too much,*
If you can fill the unforgiving minute
With sixty seconds worth of distance run,
Yours is the earth, and everything that's in it . . .

It was said of Moses, perhaps the greatest character in the Old Testament, that he was 'the meekest man in all the earth'. Certainly it was he who found his fellow countrymen a rabble and welded them into a nation, setting their feet on the course of progressive development that was to culminate in God's supreme revelation in Jesus. As we study his career, we cannot fail to notice the emergence and persistence of those qualities which we have already set forth as belonging to meekness. At the outset, we are told, he 'by faith refused to become the son of Pharoh's daughter', not because there would have been anything intrinsically dishonourable in that, but because he sensed there was other and more important work for him to do. Such a decision may be recorded in a brief sentence, but it reveals an extraordinary measure of self-control. His courage was displayed in his fearless confrontation of Pharaoh, and then ensued what must have been the severest test of all, the leadership of an often stupid and obstinate people for no less than forty years in the wilderness as they made their slow pilgrimage to the promised land. The only blemishes on his character as recorded are to be seen in those rare lapses when his meekness temporarily deserted him and he lost his temper, thereby forfeiting the privilege of sharing in the ultimate achievement of the purpose to which he had dedicated himself.

But it was, as we have come to see in each Beatitude, our Lord Himself who perfectly embodied the virtue He proclaimed. The secret of His unique life of purity and love lay first in His insight into the Father's character and purpose, and consequently in His own absolute loyalty to the part that it was the Father's will for Him to play in its fulfilment. In the story of the Temptation, we are shown in pictorial form how subtly He was tempted to seek to gain His end by methods inconsistent with His Father's character. Such temptations doubtless recurred from time to time, and we know how on occasion His own friends sought to deflect Him from the path of complete obedience, and how in the Garden of Gethsemane He faced the bitterest inward conflict of all. If He had yielded and used the devil's weapons, His career might have issued in a blaze of glory, but He would never have become the Saviour of men. But nothing caused Him to swerve from His course of undeviating loyalty to His Father's will. We see this perhaps in clearest relief when, realizing all that was involved, 'He steadfastly set his face to go to Jerusalem'.

The hymn-writer has caught the significance of

that majestic meekness in the well-known Palm Sunday hymn

O Saviour meek, pursue Thy road
With palms and scattered garments strowed.

Finally, the message He had proclaimed in word and deed in His life He proclaimed with even greater power in His sacrificial and triumphant death. On Calvary, when everyone else was carried away by some overpowering emotion, some by hate and some by fear, so that they could be said not to be themselves at the time, He was supremely Himself, fulfilling in this last dread act what the Father had given Him to do.

In this, as always, it was the character of the eternal God that He revealed. God was and is and is to be. All things were made by Him, and all things are in His hand. God can afford to wait:

. . . the slow watches of the night
Not less to God belong,
And for the everlasting right
The silent stars are strong.

In the creation of the world and of man for fellowship with Himself, we can observe God's patient processes. In His dealing with men He never coerces, but neither does He ever abandon. As Francis Thompson memorably expressed it,

> *Still with unhurrying chase,*
> *And unperturbèd pace,*
> *Deliberate speed, majestic instancy,*

He pursues men with the meekness of eternal love. Those who respond are solemnly invited to follow in His steps, and, in doing so, discover that all things are theirs, for they are Christ's and Christ is God's.

'Blessed are the meek: for they shall inherit the earth.'

THEY THAT HUNGER AND THIRST
AFTER RIGHTEOUSNESS

BLESSED are they, for they shall be filled, and filled, of course, with righteousness, not necessarily with anything else. It was not our Lord, but the Psalmist who wrote, 'I have been young and now am old; yet have I not seen the righteous forsaken, nor his seed begging their bread,' and the only appropriate comment in our world, and surely in his, would seem to be that his experience must have been singularly limited. Jesus did indeed say 'Seek ye first His Kingdom and His righteousness, and all these things shall be added unto you'; but the Kingdom tarries, and in the meantime its social blessings tarry too.

In this fourth Beatitude – unlike the first three – there is no paradox, but the application in a particular realm of a general principle which holds good throughout life: 'Ask, and it shall be given you; seek and ye shall find; knock and it shall be opened unto you.' Broadly speaking, the universe is responsive to our desires. The greatest tragedies of life do not occur because men seek and fail to find, but because they seek the wrong things and do find them, only to discover them to be a curse and not the blessing they imagined. The Bible is full of examples, but secular literature is no less so. We can all remember the kind of fairy tale we read as children, in which three wishes were granted and the first two were unwisely used with such disastrous results that the third had to be employed to restore the status quo. 'When ye pray,' said Jesus, 'ye shall not be as the hypocrites: for they love to stand and pray in the synagogues and in the corners of the streets, that they may be seen of men. Verily I say unto you, "They have received their reward."' Their prayers were not heard, but that was not their object. Their real desire was to be regarded as pious and godly men, and that aim was realized.

Human desire is here described through the metaphor of hunger and thirst. These are primary and elemental appetites, understood by everybody. Probably the reader of these pages, like the writer of them, has never felt these desires in an acute and desperate form like the hungry prodigal son in the parable or a thirsty traveller in a desert, but it is a shameful blot on our humanity that nearly half the human race, even in this modern world of plenty, do habitually suffer this experience, and we all know in a measure what it is to be hungry, even if we are fortunate enough to be able to satisfy our hunger at will. Similarly, we can recall occasions when, in other than a physical sense, all our energies of mind and heart were directed towards the satisfying of some craving or the attainment of some goal, which at the time seemed of supreme worth and importance. In such matters the maintenance of our desire is essential. Any doctor will testify to the necessity of the will to live in his patients. Similarly, Jesus' first question to the man whose eager desire had waned after thirty-eight years by the pool at Bethesda was, 'Wouldst thou be made whole?', that is, 'Do you really want to be well?'

Religious teachers and moralists have differed in the advice they have given concerning those desires which are natural to us as men and women. Buddhist religion and Stoic philosophy urge us to suppress them. All desire is to be eradicated as quickly and completely as possible. An appropriate Beatitude would appear to be 'Blessed is he that desireth nothing, for he shall not be disappointed'. The fewer our wants, the happier we shall be. Let no man pour scorn on those who have held and practised this view. They include many noble souls, and there is something fine about the austere asceticism which they display. I believe, however, that the religion of Jesus points a better way.

Less admirable is the attitude which can be summed up in the words, 'Let us eat, drink and be merry; for tomorrow we die.' Regarded superficially, the lives of many in the world today seem to be lived on this principle, but fortunately it is not for us to judge. This is an attitude, however, which is certainly characteristic of a not inconsiderable body of people who are appalled at the state of the world and feel the future holds out no worthy promise for themselves or their children. Time is short, eternity a vague surmise, and wisdom lies in satisfying all our desires to the utmost of our ability and enjoying that satisfaction while we can.

Still less, it need hardly be said, does this represent the Christian view. Jesus neither encouraged us to suppress our desires nor to give them free and unrestricted rein. Our desires, He taught, are to be directed to the right object, and then they will be fulfilled. The universe is so constructed that the instincts which are implanted in us by God are capable of being satisfied. We hunger for food, and the need can be supplied. We hunger for knowledge, and truth can be revealed. We hunger for love, and that desire too can be met. The secret of great and worthy living is to have the right desire. The Bible abounds in examples of the application of this metaphor to religious aspiration. 'As the hart panteth after the waterbrooks, so panteth my soul after Thee, O God. My soul thirsteth for God, for the living God.' 'Ho, everyone that thirsteth, come ye to the waters.' 'They shall hunger no more, neither thirst any more.' Similarly, in the fourth Gospel, our Lord in His conversation with the Samaritan woman, and in the discourse following the feeding of the five thousand, made free use of the same metaphor.

In this Beatitude, He pronounces a blessing upon those whose desires are fixed upon what should be man's supreme aim, namely righteousness. Righteousness is a conception which runs right through scripture, the Old Testament as well as the New, and this is no place to attempt an exposition of its development and its profound meaning. It is desirable, however, for our purpose to seek to disengage it from the sphere of abstruse theological thought, and relate it to the context of our ordinary lives. Righteousness, I would suggest, means rightness of a particular kind. The word 'right' is used in many different connections to denote 'what ought to be'. Some of these connections are quite trivial. We may say, for example, about the arrangement of furniture in a room, or flowers in a bowl, that it is 'right'. Similarly, an artist referring to his picture, or a preacher to his sermon, may say 'I couldn't get it *right*'. Something about it offends and cries out to be remedied. In every instance, what is meant is that it ought to be different, and we cannot rest until it is different and 'right'. Righteousness has something of this meaning applied to character, what we are, and conduct, how we behave. The *New English Bible* recognized this in its rendering, 'How blest are those who hunger and thirst to see right prevail'. The man who is blessed in this respect is the man who above all desires to fulfil the intention of his being and become what he ought to be.

But how is this desire to be acquired? Can a man hunger and thirst after righteousness to order? The answer is that this holy desire has been planted in our personalities as surely as the desire for food and drink. It may have been displaced by unworthy desires, its intensity may have been diminished almost to vanishing point by persistent neglect, but it is there. In every man, side by side with the desires of which he is conscious and which are dominant for the moment, there is the voice which says, 'I ought'. It expresses itself through the faculty which we call conscience, which can be warped and blunted, but which is never extinguished. By this he is enabled to distinguish between right and wrong. Deep down, and often

E

overlaid with sinful desires which he has allowed to control him, there is the desire to become what he by nature was intended to be. Moses reminded the children of Israel of this when he exhorted them, 'This commandment which I command thee this day, it is not too hard for thee, neither is it far off. It is not in heaven that thou shouldest say, "Who shall go up to heaven, and bring it unto us, and make us to hear it, that we may do it?" Neither is it beyond the sea, that thou shouldest say, "Who shall go over the sea for us, and bring it unto us, and make us to hear it, that we may do it?" But the word is very nigh unto thee, in thy mouth and in thy heart, that thou mayest do it.'

Furthermore, alike in individuals and in society there is broad general agreement as to what *is* right and what *is* wrong. The whole ordering of society rests on the existence of this common mind within the community. If it disappeared chaos would ensue. Even at a time like the present when time-honoured moral standards are challenged or ignored, the question men ask is not usually 'What is good?' but 'Why should I be good in a world like this?' This fact reinforces the Christian view that the character and purpose of God are the ultimate sanctions for right behaviour, and once again we come to see that this Beatitude only comes alive as it is seen not as an abstract moral precept but in the light of our Lord's revelation of that character and purpose.

Our conscience when persistently violated becomes blunted and less sensitive, but never entirely stilled. To hunger and thirst after righteousness means that the desires of our heart are in harmony with the inner voice of conscience; and the promise of the Beatitude is that, when that is so, God, the Giver of all good things, who supplies the needs of our bodies and our minds, is pledged to fulfil this deepest need of all. This divine willingness to satisfy our longings is clearly illustrated in the parables of the friend at midnight and the importunate widow. These parables are misunderstood if they are interpreted as portraying God as reluctant to hear our prayers or grudging in answering them. The truth they convey is the necessity of earnest and persistent entreaty. 'Prayer is the soul's sincere desire', and God, who bestows so many gifts with lavish generosity, whether we recognize the Giver or not, making His sun to rise on the evil and the good and sending rain on the just and the unjust, reserves His supreme spiritual blessings for those who, conscious of their need, turn to Him in faith, like children to their earthly fathers whom they trust. If we have not received them, we have not wanted them desperately enough. This withholding on God's part is for our sakes, in order that through life's discipline we may make the supreme discovery that we belong to Him and that our blessedness springs from a recognition of that glorious truth. 'Thou hast made us for Thyself, and our hearts are restless until they find their rest in Thee.' Whenever a man shares God's purpose with eager desire, a new way is opened whereby God's power is released in him and through him. Such eager desire, a hunger and thirst after righteousness, is an indispensable element, if God's will is to be done.

This discovery delivers us also from all anxiety about merit. God's requirements are infinite, and our duty is measureless, but so are the divine resources available to us. We must needs be unprofitable servants, since God's purpose for us is nothing short of perfection. This no man could ever achieve or deserve, but it is the gift of God. It is the goal to which we advance in so far as we trust Him and commit ourselves to Him, and discipleship is not a ceaseless striving to meet a terrifying and impossible demand, but a joyous pilgrimage to the goal of God's purpose.

'Beloved, now are we children of God, and it is not yet made manifest what we shall be. We know that if He shall be manifested we shall be like Him; for we shall see Him even as He is.'

'Blessed are they that hunger and thirst after righteousness: for they shall be filled.'

THE MERCIFUL

ALL the Beatitudes involve our relationship with our fellows, but none more directly and obviously so than this one, in which a blessing is pronounced upon the merciful. The situation envisaged is one in which, through wrongdoing or failure of some other kind, another human being is in our power. How are we going to treat him? Will his deserts or his needs prove the decisive factor? Will consideration of personal advantage, including maybe the satisfaction of natural resentment, determine our attitude, or will Paul's advice prevail, 'If thine enemy hunger, feed him; if he thirst, give him to drink'? The same issue faces the community in its dealings with offenders. Is the defence of society or the reclamation of the criminal to be the guiding principle?

In the earlier group of Beatitudes, it was possible to examine the qualities set forth, poverty of spirit, mourning and meekness, at the human level, and then to see how these qualities were perfectly embodied in Jesus, who revealed thereby the character of God. But to regard this second group as if they were merely moral precepts is impossible from the outset. The unbeliever might find some meaning in the earlier group solely on an ethical basis, but it is difficult to see what sense he could extract from these later ones. Righteousness and purity may have some meaning for the atheist, but it would be so completely different in content from the meaning they convey to the believer in God that it would be purposeless to consider it here. Similarly, mercy is inseparably associated in our minds with the activity of God. 'To err is human, to forgive divine', wrote Alexander Pope. Again, Shakespeare even more definitely asserts of mercy,

> '*It is an attribute of God Himself,*
> *And earthly power doth then show likest God's*
> *When mercy seasons justice.*'

It follows that we shall most surely arrive at the meaning of this Beatitude if we approach it from the standpoint of the mercy of God towards undeserving sinners, which is at the heart of the gospel. It is because it is in harmony with the character and gracious activity of God that it is incumbent also on us.

Furthermore, by this approach, we shall best resolve, as far as with our limited minds we are able to resolve, the problem that so often bedevils human attempts to grapple with the moral issues involved in forgiveness, namely the apparent inconsistency between mercy and justice. Even Shakespeare allowed himself to set these two principles in opposition when, in the passage quoted above, he spoke of mercy 'seasoning' justice. But God is altogether merciful and altogether just, and any seeming antinomy must be due to the narrow range of our human perception.

What the mercy of God is in fact opposed to is a low and mechanical idea of justice, which has even found its way into some theories of the atonement. What the justice of God is opposed to is a shallow and unreal interpretation of mercy as a cheap benevolence. God is love. He is always love, not sometimes love and sometimes something else. God cannot deny Himself. Sometimes the love of God expresses itself in wrath, the wrath which 'is revealed from heaven against all ungodliness and unrighteousness of men.' The system of things under which we live is one where there is a ceaseless and unrelenting reaction against evil. No view could be more damnable than that which regards sin lightly. If a man sins, suffering is an inescapable consequence, indeed a whole train of consequences may be set in motion. Similarly on a world scale, if international or economic relationships are based on wrong foundations, distress and misery inevitably occur. This world is a world under judgement. If men refuse God's grace, they will experience His wrath. This, however, is no denial of God's love, but an expression of it: 'Whom the Lord loveth He chasteneth.' Mr C. S. Lewis has described these judgements of God as a 'flag of truth planted in a rebel fortress'. Just as many a man's life has been saved by a pain which has warned him of something amiss in his physical state, so God punishes, not out of vindictiveness but in order to win men back to His way of truth and righteousness.

God's punishments, however, are never arbitrary. They follow in the wake of sin as effect follows cause. As virtue is its own reward, so sin is its own punishment. In God's world, which will only work His way, such bitter consequences of sin are inevitable. It would, indeed, be a godless world if men or nations could flout His will and all remain comfortable. But God never abandons us in our sin; He seeks always to unveil us to ourselves, as we already appear to Him.

But justice as dispensed by men is at best rough and blundering justice. When men reward and punish, there is no inherent connection between the deed and the consequence. A mother may promise her child a chocolate for good behaviour while he is bathed, but there is no necessary connection between the chocolate and the bath. Similarly, in the penal system, there is a scale of arbitrary penalties varying with the heinousness of the crime.

The acid test whereby the rightness of human justice may be measured is its purpose. We may thankfully recognize that much progress has been made in this respect in recent times, but much remains to be done. Too often still, human punishment tends to degrade rather than reform. Many more competent than I would claim on both ethical and religious grounds that there must be a retributive element in punishment. They may be right, although I fail to discern it in God's dealings with men as far as I can observe them. The protection of society may also be a necessary subsidiary concern, but what is beyond the slightest doubt from a Christian point of view is that the main object of punishment inflicted by man should be to redeem and transform the wrongdoer. This is the ultimate condemnation of capital punishment, which is a confession of failure on society's part. Too often men seem obsessed with the idea that justice is concerned with what has happened instead of what is going to happen. Some abstract principle of justice must be vindicated, and those who have violated it must be made to smart for the sake of it. But God is concerned with the future. He recognizes our sin and never condones it, but He seeks to save us from it. This is the meaning of the incarnation and the redemptive death of our Lord.

So far was God from vindictiveness or desire for vengeance that He became man to avert our final ruin. Being willing neither to abandon us nor to compromise with us, He identified Himself in a redeeming way with our sin. Our sin was His shame, our suffering His sorrow, and our redemption His satisfaction.

He died that we might be forgiven,
He died to make us good.

So the New Testament tells us, 'If we confess our sins, He is faithful and just to forgive us our sins.' The natural adjective we should expect according to our human way of reckoning would not be 'just' but 'merciful'. But in the divine character there is no inconsistency between justice and mercy. When the love of God wins from us the recognition of our sins as the evil things they are, and a true repentance, no further obstacle remains, and the door is open for forgiveness and our restoration to fellowship with God.

Mercy, however, is the concern of us all, not only because it is something within our power as individuals and as members of the community to give or to withhold, but also because it is a primary need of our own.

> 'Consider this
> That in the course of justice none of us
> Should see salvation : we do pray for mercy
> And that same power doth teach us all to render
> The deeds of mercy.'

The blessing our Lord pronounces on the merciful is that they themselves shall obtain mercy. Here is no spiritual bargain with God as if the Beatitude ran, 'Blessed are they that overlook the sins of others: for their own shall be overlooked.' We have already seen that such an attitude to sin would be morally disastrous. Rather does this promise lead us to a truth that is at the heart of the gospel. Few truths are given greater prominence in our Lord's teaching. It recurs again and again. Forgiveness is the free gift of God to undeserving men and women; it can neither be earned nor bought. But only those who are themselves forgiving are able to receive it. So He taught us to pray, 'Forgive us, as we forgive.' In the parables, notably the story of the unmerciful servant and the story of the prodigal son, He emphasizes the same truth. This is no arbitrary condition God chooses to impose, but is inherent in a man's relationships with God and his fellows. The moral laws of the universe make it impossible for us to receive the forgiveness of God and refuse our own. The Kingdom of God is a Kingdom of right relationships. It is the family of God into which we are brought as forgiven sinners. By entering that family we come into a new relationship not only to God but also to all the other members. So the elder brother in the familiar story, being unwilling to sit at meat with his scapegrace brother now returned home, was by that very fact excluded from the Father's house. The door was open, the Father besought him, but his own unforgiving spirit made it impossible.

The gospel narrative makes it clear that Jesus had comparatively little difficulty in dealing with sinners who were conscious of their need of forgiveness, but very great difficulty with people who had opportunities to forgive but were unwilling to do so. This is so central in our Lord's teaching that it would seem that more people remain outside the Kingdom because they are unforgiving than because they are unwilling to receive forgiveness. In human relationships forgiveness is the cement which binds communities together. More homes are wrecked by unwillingness to forgive than by the wrongdoing of those who need to be forgiven. The absence of the spirit of forgiveness between nations needs no underlining. We talk glibly about international justice, which is indeed an admirable ideal, but mercy between man and man is the crying need. Only when men learn to display in their dealings with each other that mercy which God has shown to them in Jesus Christ can we hope for the real and lasting peace for which men yearn.

Such an attitude is not the prerogative of the casual or easygoing but of those who recognize the cost of redemptive love and are ready to pay it.

> *O man, forgive thy mortal foe*
> *Nor ever strike him blow for blow,*
> *For all the saints on earth that live*
> *To be forgiven must forgive,*
> *For all the blessed souls in heaven*
> *Are both forgivers and forgiven.*

'Blessed are the merciful: for they shall obtain mercy.'

THE PURE IN HEART

THIS is the crown of the Beatitudes. Those we have already considered lead up to it. Those which follow derive from it. It has a special significance for our present study, in that we see here how in the Christian scheme of things religion and morality are inseparable. The goal of all religion is to see God. All the ethical virtues find their consummation in purity of heart. The ever present danger, attending all moral effort and concern, is the concentration of interest upon ourselves. Even the salutary self-examination commended by Paul may have the effect of preventing that self-forgetfulness which is essential to true religion. The chief end of man, as the Scots have taught us, is to glorify God and enjoy Him for ever. This has important ethical implications, as we are concerned to draw out here, but if our attention is fastened on ourselves doing right and becoming good, if thought about ourselves ousts thought about God, our moral and spiritual activity are both vitiated. In so far as we succeed in attaining any ethical standard we shall be in danger of spiritual pride; in so far as we fall short, of spiritual despair. In either event we shall be living in a thought-world governed by considerations of merit, from which the grace of hungering and thirsting after righteousness, as we have already seen, should have delivered us.

Who then are the pure in heart to whom the vision of God is promised? Quite obviously, we must relate our interpretation to the rest of our Lord's teaching, which means that purity of heart is a grace God is willing to bestow upon everybody. It is not something reserved for a select few. There have been and still are those who find it possible to withdraw from time to time from the contamination of this evil world and, oblivious of time and sense, become absorbed in contemplation of a beatific vision of surpassing radiance. Such people appear to enjoy an immediate experience of God, whereas for most of us our experience is mediated. The reality of such experiences cannot be questioned, nor can their value, both for those who have them and for others. But mysticism of that particular kind is a mark of temperament rather than of sanctity, and is not what is referred to here.

Equally surely, this is not a pronouncement of blessing on the respectable. The purity concerned is not synonymous with an upright and blameless character, a refraining from all lust and loathsome sins. This will, of course, be involved, but is a much too restricted and superficial conception of purity. We only need to consider the Pharisees to realize this. They were not bad men pretending to be good, but good men, measured by any merely ethical standard, whose very goodness blinded their eyes to the vision of God.

The word 'pure' primarily denotes 'unmixed'. Pure gold is gold without alloy. Pure water is water free from any other liquid or matter. So purity of heart is often interpreted as singlemindedness. This seems to me to be an admirable interpretation so long as we bear in mind that it means singlemindedness in devotion to God. The expression 'pure in heart' has no verbal parallel in our Lord's teaching, but He did say 'If thine eye be single, thine whole body shall be full of light', and it is our organ of spiritual vision which needs to be single if we are to see God. Whether we see God depends not on God but on ourselves. It is not enough for an object to be there for us to see it; it is also necessary for our vision to be unimpaired. This is presumably what is meant by the expression 'Beauty is in the eye of the beholder', as is certainly implied in our Lord's references to those who have eyes but see not. An artist will see something in a landscape which the rest of us do not see, though, as we too have eyes, he can help us to see it. If we ask a number of people who have travelled the same road to describe it, their accounts will differ because they will all have seen, or failed to see, various things on the route. To a large extent, the things we see are determined by the things we look for.

'Pussy cat, pussy cat, where have you been?'
'I've been to London to visit the Queen.'
'Pussy cat, pussy cat, what saw you there?'
'I saw a little mouse under a chair.'

Not the splendour of the court, nor even the Queen herself, but only the little mouse had attracted the cat's attention. That was all it was really interested in.

Hence we are confronted in the gospels with the extraordinary paradox that when God became man, those whose spiritual vision was blinded failed to see God in Him. The religious leaders of His people were so dismayed by the threat to their privileges and prerogatives that even His purity failed to rebuke them. 'He came unto His own, and they that were His own received Him not.' He, on the other hand, in whom the organ of spiritual vision was undimmed, saw something of inestimable worth in the woman of the streets, in the corrupt tax gatherer, and in His enemies who crucified Him. So sin cheats and blinds us. We see everything but God, and miss the meaning and significance of life.

The psychologists help us to understand single-mindedness. The word they often use to describe it is integration. We are accustomed to regard ourselves as individuals. Each of us is a self, and it is that self which, for example, sees and hears and experiences hunger. In this sense we each stand out distinctly from the community to which we belong; and although we sometimes think of a flock of sheep taking fright or a nation feeling some intense emotion, we know that this only happens if the individual sheep and the individual citizens undergo the experience. But there is also a sense in which each individual is several selves rolled into one. As I have said in another place, we are made up of different instincts and impulses seeking expression and ranging themselves around different ideals, some of our own choosing and some taken for granted. 'So-and-so is a different man at business from what he is at home.' Who has not heard that kind of thing said, and rightly said? It need not mean that the man in question is insincere, but rather that he has not yet brought his ideals into harmony. All of us have tried at some time or other to excuse ourselves by saying, 'I wasn't myself when I did that.' But if I wasn't myself, who was I? What we mean is that we weren't at that moment the particular self we should like people to imagine as our true self. Most of us know what it is to be torn and distracted within ourselves as we try to follow inconsistent ideals. We resemble an army where every soldier marches in a direction of his own. Our personalities are in need of integration. This integration occurs when we discover some object in life big enough and compelling enough to mould into a unity the discordant elements in our nature.

We all experience this for limited periods, when all our interest and energy is unreservedly concentrated for the time being on some activity. At such times we are entirely happy, but these occasions pass and our continuing need is for some worthy aim in pursuit of which the many sides of our nature can find fulfilment and to which they can be utterly devoted.

In the Christian view the only object fulfilling these requirements is God Himself, revealed in Jesus Christ. The qualities of the individual are personal, and they need a person as the object of their devotion. Ideals can achieve much, but in the end no impersonal ideal is compelling enough.

F

Only love can win from men a complete response to its demands, and only answering love in men can sustain that response. Part of the genius of the Christian religion is that it is centred in a Person whose claims on His followers are absolute, admitting of no compromise. This is the explanation of some of our Lord's sayings that startle by their sternness. 'He that loveth father or mother more than me is not worthy of me.' There may be other loyalties, but they must be subordinate and must never be allowed to clash with the one all-inclusive loyalty. Richard Lovelace expresses this spirit in the well known couplet:

> *I could not love thee, dear, so much,*
> *Loved I not honour more.*

When such a reorientation of our whole being takes place, and God in Jesus Christ becomes the object of our worship and His service the dominant passion of our lives, the result is what is described in the New Testament as being born anew or being a new creation. Such is the extent of the change involved.

The reason that the vision of most of us is blurred is not that God is hiding Himself. On the contrary, He is seeking us. But we have not been prepared to recognize His absolute claim. We have held back from the complete surrender His love requires if this crowning blessing is to be ours. But the promise of our Lord is clear and it is universal: the pure in heart see God.

They see Him supremely as they gaze on Jesus,

but they see Him everywhere. For the pure in heart nature is the garment of the living God.

Heaven above is softer blue,
Earth around is sweeter green,
Something lives in every hue
Christless eyes have never seen.

Similarly, the unfolding purpose of God and His divine Lordship are discerned by the pure in heart as they contemplate the pageant of history with its achievements and its disasters. For the pure in heart all the discipline of life ministers to God's gracious and loving purpose. As our Lord Himself, in the circumstances created by the malice and hatred of His enemies, perceived the will of the Father and obeyed it, so the pure in heart discover that to them that love God all things, not a selection of things, work together for good.

It is well, however, to remind ourselves that this purity of heart is not a separate quality alongside the earlier ones, but is the climax which includes them all in perfect balance. It is the gift of God to those who acknowledge God's absolute claim on their souls.

Perhaps the best commentary on this Beatitude is to be found in the first epistle of John: 'Beloved, now are we children of God, and it is not yet made manifest what we shall be. We know that if He shall be manifested we shall be like Him; for we shall see Him even as He is.'

THE PEACEMAKERS

THIS Beatitude strikes a responsive chord in every heart. It brings us face to face with the supreme task confronting humanity in this generation. The happiness of mankind in the foreseeable future, and perhaps the future itself of mankind, depends on its fulfilment. Probably there is nobody in the world today who desires war. We all want peace, however unwilling we may be to pursue those policies which will ensure it. In spite of the repeated failure of men to establish and maintain lasting peace, we cherish the hope that we shall succeed where earlier generations have failed. This hope sustains us in a day when continued failure must result in irretrievable disaster.

For the purposes of this study, however, the very urgency of this matter constitutes a danger. Our consideration must begin, not with the concrete situation in which we find ourselves, however important that may be, but with the place this Beatitude occupies in the picture our Lord is drawing. Only so shall we discover the relevance of this saying to contemporary events.

The ideal character our Lord has been building up is nearing its completion. This is the last Beatitude which sets forth a quality of character. Indeed, even here it might be urged that peacemaking denotes an activity rather than a quality. It is, however, an activity through which a certain quality of character finds expression. Furthermore, it comes appropriately at the end, as it is an activity which includes all the qualities already laid down and embodies a whole attitude to life.

Looking back over the catalogue of qualities contained in the Beatitudes, we can observe significance in their order. They display a steady progression. Beginning with poverty of spirit, which, as we have seen, involves a sense of need without which it is not possible for us to receive God's gifts at all, the list proceeds through mourning for sin, meekness, hunger and thirst after righteousness, a merciful spirit, to its crown, that purity of heart which brings a vision of God. A little reflection will serve to show that one blessing that virtue brings in its train is the blessing of peace. Utter surrender to God and recognition of His absolute claim on us means the disappearance of the warring element in our souls. Conflicting desires are harmonized and all our powers are devoted to God. However wide and varied our activities, we can say with Paul, 'This one thing I do.'

The result is peace, which, as it is not dependent on outward circumstances, the world can neither give nor take away. It is the gift of God, the peace which passes all understanding.

Our Lord Himself possessed it and bestowed it upon His disciples. 'My peace I leave with you.' He spoke these words as He left them to face the supreme spiritual conflict in all history. He entrusted them with the carrying on of His work, involving persecution, shame and death, but with that trust He left them too this legacy of peace.

As He shared it with them, so they were commissioned to share it with others. It is God's gift, offered to and intended for the world. No man can hug it to himself, as if it were exclusively bestowed upon a chosen few. Only as we share it, do we continue to possess it. He who has the peace of God must needs express it in the activity of peacemaking. It is an inner quality which fortifies the soul against the world, but at the same time it is an atmosphere into which the world is to be brought. Like the gospel itself, of which it is a fruit, it is in its essence missionary.

The only peace which can meet the needs of men, or match their hopes, is the peace of God, since it is the only peace which rests upon reality.

What is the cause of war? Many answers are given to that question. Frontier disputes, trade rivalry, national prestige are among them. These are important matters and have played their part at different times. But they are occasions of war rather than its cause, and, as such, are relatively superficial. The roots of war lie further down in the human soul than we care to think. The conditions of peace are the same for nations as for individuals, namely recognition and acceptance of the sovereignty of God. The truth is that this is God's world. Men and nations alike who treat it as a world to be manipulated in their selfish interests are attempting to live in a world which does not exist.

As there are warring elements within our individual personalities, so humanity itself is torn by many differences of race, colour, language, political theory, economic status, and, underlying them all, the difference of sex on which the whole social fabric rests. These differences are not to be denied. They are real. They might prove enriching, but all too often they issue in conflict. Deeper and more abiding than these differences is the solidarity of the human race. God made man in His own image, and He made of one blood all the nations of the earth. Peacemaking involves nothing less than the laying hold of this amazing world, with its newly discovered and breathtaking resources, and its complex network of relationships, and dedicating it to the glory of God. That is the only principle big enough to unify the otherwise hopelessly conflicting aspirations and ambitions of mankind. This depends on a recognition that it is God's world. If it is regarded as man's world, it will be a prize to be fought over and seized by the strongest for their own selfish desires, and the end of that, as of all illusions, is frustration and chaos.

So the task of the followers of Jesus is to reconcile man to God, and thereby men to one another. Their ministry, like that of their Lord, is a ministry of reconciliation.

For the first three centuries the Christian Church was peacemaking in this sense. Perhaps the deepest of all Paul's insights, at a time when the young Christian religion was confined to a few centres of population in Europe and Asia Minor, was his recognition that in Christ every barrier between men, be it of race, of economic status or of sex, is done away. 'There can be neither Jew nor

Greek, there can be neither bond nor free, there can be no male nor female: for ye all are one man in Christ Jesus.' So in Corinth and in Ephesus, in Philippi and in Rome, the early Christian community was a cross section of the whole population. Broadly speaking, the Christian Church remained peacemaking for three centuries. Only when the Emperor Constantine was converted and Christianity became the official religion of the Roman Empire was this universality of the Christian family weakened. The task today, in a world where modern science has bound mankind in close and inescapable contact, is to reaffirm that original insight, and make it actual in political and economic relationships.

In the light of this, the positive nature of peace becomes apparent. No great word of the New Testament is so little understood. Nobody ever suggests that truth is merely abstention from falsehood, or righteousness abstention from evil. But it is a commonplace to hear peace described in such a way that it is clearly regarded as the absence of war. In this sense there are many spurious forms of peace. So-called peace may be imposed by conquest, may be the result of indifference between next door neighbours, may depend upon compromise after the imperfect patching up of a quarrel, or, as at present in the international field, may be based on mutual fear. The peace of our world today is a peace not made but precariously kept. It has to be preserved with ceaseless vigilance like a delicate and fragile piece of china, lest the unleashing of the devilish forces of destruction turn the earth into one vast graveyard, where peace is the peace of death.

But the peace of God is a positive thing, to be expressed in music rather than in silence; it resembles an orchestra rather than a cemetery. It happens whenever men respond to the love of God, and so love one another with the love of which He has made them capable. It comes not by restraining men but by uniting them. It takes shape whenever men's powers find full and free expression, their varied talents and abilities being used to the glory of God and subordinated to the one supreme ideal of His Kingdom.

Towards this all-embracing ideal this Beatitude invites us to make our contribution and so approve ourselves as sons of God. All of us are doing it or failing to do it. It is not one task among many, but involves our whole attitude to life. By our very presence we help to create harmony or discord at every point at which we touch life and in every company to which we belong. This is true of us as individuals and supremely true of the Church, which is entrusted with the ministry of reconciliation. In the world we are bidden as Christians to love our enemies. This may of necessity be a unilateral activity, but in the Church we may love one another. The world, where the influence of the Church seems sometimes negligible, would not remain indifferent in the face of a Church which in its life demonstrated what all society will be like when it accepts the Lordship of Christ as the Church professes to do.

Let us be under no delusion. This is no task for

the sentimental or the easygoing. It is for the disciples of Jesus, who 'made peace by the blood of His Cross'. In war, as many can testify in different parts of the globe, outstanding examples of heroism and self-sacrifice reveal the inborn capacity of the human spirit. But the adventure of peace-making calls for even more complete devotion in the realm of thought and of action. The tasks of peace are harder than those of war. It is easier to defeat an enemy than to defeat his enmity, easier to stop a quarrel than to heal it.

Who is sufficient for these things? No man in his own strength, but those who, conscious of utter dependence on God, and seeking no end but His glory, become the agents of His perfect peace.

'Blessed are the peacemakers: for they shall be called sons of God.'

THE PERSECUTED

OUR Lord's picture of the happy man is now complete. This concluding Beatitude is of a different order. It pronounces blessedness on a man not because of what he is or what he does, but in and through the experience of persecution which inevitably befalls the faithful disciples. Jesus makes this abundantly clear by first of all enunciating the general principle, and then applying it to His immediate hearers: 'Blessed are they which are persecuted for righteousness' sake: for theirs is the kingdom of heaven. Blessed are ye, when men shall revile you, and persecute you, and shall say all manner of evil against you falsely, for my sake.'

We have noted already how the virtues extolled in the Beatitudes run counter to popular maxims and generally accepted behaviour. Our Lord counsels humility, for example, in a proud world, meekness in a self assertive world, mercy in a world which believes in vengeance, and peacemaking in a world which relies on the rude arbitrament of force. He was, however, not only the loftiest but the most practical of teachers and He knew full well what was involved for His disciples, as for Himself, in the practice of such virtues. Not only here, but on other occasions, He warns men of the consequences attendant upon discipleship in a world like this. It is a somewhat disturbing commentary on some types of latter day

evangelism, which exploit all manner of ingen-
ious devices in an endeavour to persuade men, to
reflect that our Lord on more than one occasion
appears to have deterred them. Clearly, He was
more concerned with the quality of His disciples
than with their number, and suggested that it
might be better not to begin the course rather than
to turn back after putting one's hand to the plough.
To a scribe who promised to follow Him wherever
He went, He replied, 'The foxes have holes and the
birds of the heaven have nests; but the Son of
Man hath not where to lay His head.' To the sons
of Zebedee, who asked to sit on His right and left
hand in His glory, He replied, 'Ye know not what
ye ask. Are ye able to drink the cup that I drink?'

In this Beatitude, however, our Lord asserts that
this experience, if borne for righteousness' sake,
will prove to be fraught with blessing. Not all
persecution brings such blessing in its train.
There are always those who appear to seek unpop-
ularity for its own sake, deriving a morbid satisfaction from being pilloried. They assume that the
majority must always be wrong, and take good care
never to be found among them. But our Lord did
not say, 'Blessed are the cantankerous.' Others
incur persecution, not by virtues which transcend
conventional standards but by wickedness which
falls below them. There were three crosses on
Calvary, but only one man hung there for righteousness' sake. 'We receive the due reward of our
deeds,' confessed one of the others to his com-
panion, 'but this man hath done nothing amiss.'

Furthermore, it is most important to recognize

that persecution in itself brings no blessing. On the contrary it is always a most unpleasant and disagreeable thing. There is no merit whatever in self-denial of any kind for its own sake, let alone the self-denial which issues in martyrdom. It was not for the joy of the Cross, but 'for the joy that was set before Him', which in the existing circumstances could only come by the way of the Cross, that our Lord 'endured the Cross, despising the shame'. He accepted that way because there was no other.

But although persecution does not invariably bring a blessing, no one can tread the path of discipleship without undergoing it in some form or other. There is no need to stress at any length how literally and terribly this word of Jesus was illustrated by His own fate and that of those to whom it was immediately addressed. The most damning indictment that can ever be made against humanity is that, when the character set forth in the Beatitudes was perfectly embodied in the person of our Lord Himself, all that decent men and women could do with Him was to crucify Him. The perpetrators of that crime were not horrible monsters but respected leaders in Church and State, animated by the kind of motive that animates most of us, and acting in defence of values and standards which they believed must be defended at whatever cost. Similarly with many Christians in the early centuries. 'They shall put you out of the synagogues', Jesus had warned them; 'The hour cometh, that whosoever killeth you shall think that he offereth service unto God.' If in this way our

Lord predicted the tragedy of religious persecution, which is such a blot on the nineteen centuries of Christian history, we need hardly be surprised that from many other sources, such as the godless Roman Empire in the first century and pagan totalitarian states in the twentieth, persecution has been the lot of the Christian disciple. Those of us who have never been subjected to such a test, and cannot by any stretch of the imagination picture ourselves standing firm under it, are lost in awe and wonder as we contemplate the heroism of our fathers in the faith.

> *Mocked, imprisoned, stoned, tormented,*
> *Sawn asunder, slain with sword,*
> *They have conquered death and Satan*
> *By the might of Christ the Lord.*
> *Gladly, Lord, with Thee they suffered,*
> *Gladly, Lord, with Thee they died. . . .'*

When Christopher Wordsworth penned those words he believed himself to be describing an age gone for ever. The lions, the stake and the sword were no more. Such persecution, however, and such heroism have had their counterpart in some of the continental countries of Europe in the events of the last thirty years.

In my country and in yours, and indeed in any place where these words are likely to be read, it is different. While we recognize this and should be thankful for it, let it not be supposed that persecution does not exist. If Jesus came to Britain or Australia today He would most certainly not be crucified. It is equally certain that He would be as definitely rejected as in first-century Palestine. His hands and feet would be free from blood, but His heart would bleed over the cities of our countries as bitterly as over Jerusalem nineteen centuries ago. Unimaginable as was His physical suffering, what caused His deepest agony was the sin of those who rejected Him. Moreover, the tolerance which prevails today is displayed not only towards Christians but by them. Tolerance so easily degenerates into indifference. The immunity from persecution which we enjoy is in part at any rate a consequence of our own tolerance of, and not infrequently compromise with, the paganism of the world. Such an attitude was quite foreign to our Lord, who with all His breadth of sympathy and understanding was yet narrow as a razor's edge where principles were involved. Jesus calls men to a faith and life utterly opposed to the way of the world. It is, therefore, still true that every man who, responding to that call, acknowledges our Lord's claim and pledges his fealty will of necessity meet active opposition. Such opposition may manifest itself in any one of a thousand ways. Our inherited tendencies, the environment in which we live our lives, the people we associate with at home or at work, our native endowments, our aspirations, and many other factors combine to create the occasions in which we find ourselves involved in a conflict for righteousness. Although many of these threats come from without, the battle is always won or lost in our own soul. There is the place of decision. The promise of this

Beatitude is that in facing the opposition and bearing the persecution true happiness may be found. Not the persecution but the enduring of it is fraught with blessing. The way of the Beatitudes is a hard way, but those who shun it miss the blessing. No one who displays any of the virtues of the Beatitudes ever regrets doing so, or feels the cost has been too great. No one has ever met evil with good or hatred with love and afterwards wished he had done otherwise. No one feels remorse for having suffered for righteousness' sake. On the contrary, like the suffering servant of Isaiah 53, his reward is to 'see of the travail of his soul and be satisfied'. The reward is not in any outward or visible compensation, but in the blessedness of a life lived under the rule of God, in fellowship with Him.

So the last Beatitude links up with the first. In the first the Kingdom of Heaven is promised to the poor in spirit, those who are aware of their great need and so are able to accept the blessed rule of God and dwell in His Kingdom. In the last it is promised to those who, themselves redeemed by the Lord Jesus Christ, are counted worthy of the supreme privilege of being His instruments, and of themselves bearing some small part of the cost whereby His rule is manifested in power and made effective in the world.

'Blessed are they that are persecuted for righteousness' sake: for theirs is the Kingdom of Heaven.'

PART THREE

CONCLUSION

CONCLUSION

WE have now completed our review of the teaching of Jesus, based on the Beatitudes. In the course of this review, we have been able time and again to note similar teaching in other sections of the gospels, notably the parables, so that we are justified in affirming that the Beatitudes present us in succinct form with a sample of our Lord's teaching which is both representative and characteristic. Before proceeding, however, to draw conclusions from this, it would be well to consider how far we can assume that the gospels in their present form contain a trustworthy account of what Jesus taught. In this connection, two questions call for examination.

(a) Biblical scholarship has made great strides within the lifetime of many present-day Christians, and it is difficult to realize what a revolutionary and sometimes disturbing effect the necessary adjustment to this new knowledge has produced. As recently as the beginning of this century, the overwhelming majority of worshipping Christians took it for granted that in reading those portions of the gospels which contain the teaching of our Lord they were reading what our Lord actually said in the circumstances there described. In these days, when the findings of Biblical scholars have been popularized in books which are easily accessible to all and in talks on the radio, such naïve beliefs

have been discarded except by incorrigible literal-
ists. It is recognized that there is probably no
single extant saying which can be attributed to our
Lord with absolute certainty. For some people the
first result of this was devastating, even to the
extent of undermining their faith. Further reflection, however, should not only dispel this alarm
but bring positive reassurance.

Reliance on the verbal text of the gospel was
never a firm foundation for faith. When challenged, thoughtful people would be compelled to
admit that the Bible in English, or any modern
language for that matter, was twice removed from
the actual speech of Jesus. The Aramaic He used
was translated into the Greek of the original
gospels, and later translated again into the modern
tongue. It is not, however, merely a matter of two
translations. The earliest gospel was not composed
for at least twenty years after the events described,
and it is most unlikely that any part of our Lord's
teaching was written down during His lifetime.
The early Church believed that the end of the
world was approaching and there was therefore no
need for a permanent record of that kind. But
stories about Jesus, and stories He had told and
sayings He had uttered were current among them
from the beginning. When the first generation of
followers began to die out and the young Christian
Church continued to make its way in a world that
did not come to an end, the need for a written
account was recognized. The gospels as we have
them show how that need was met. This is not the
place to give a detailed account of how the different

gospels came to have their present form. Many such accounts in readable and understandable form are available to all. But an appreciation of the sequence of events, as briefly outlined above, far from undermining men's faith in their trustworthiness, should commend them to the discerning reader. Incidentally, if there were modifications made as the stories and sayings were handed on from one to another, such changes are less likely in the sayings of our Lord than in any other part of the narrative. Furthermore, we are faced with the sayings as they are. If they are not authentic utterances of Jesus, we must attribute them to some other teacher, of whose existence there is not the slightest hint. That is a wildly improbable conjecture.

The Christian movement owes its origin to Jesus of Nazareth whose mighty works are recorded in the gospel. It was the impact of His whole personality on His contemporaries which brought Him into conflict with the leaders of His own country, who saw in Him a threat to the ancient religious traditions of which they were the guardians. All the evidence points to the fact that from the beginning His words constituted as potent a factor as His deeds in provoking the opposition of the authorities. Hence it was natural that His teaching should be remembered and that in due course it should be recorded. That is what occurred.

The earliest of our gospels, that of Mark, is a narrative of the events of His ministry leading to His death and resurrection. It contained very little teaching. The gospels of Matthew and Luke used Mark as the basis of their accounts, and inserted groups of our Lord's sayings but in different ways. In Luke's gospel they are scattered throughout the narrative in appropriate places, whereas in Matthew they are collected into larger sections. It is in one such section, the longest of them all, filling three chapters and known as the Sermon on the Mount, that we find the Beatitudes in the version we have been considering. Thus in these sayings the teaching of our Lord has been set forth in orderly and formal fashion, but there is no evidence whatever that its meaning has been twisted. Everything points the other way. At the end of the Sermon on the Mount the very significant comment is made that 'He taught them as one having authority and not as their scribes'. But wherein did this authority reside? Not in any external sanction, nor in any official position held by the Teacher. It was a very different kind of authority from that to which His hearers were accustomed. It resided partly in the intrinsic truth of the teaching itself which winged its way into the hearts and consciences of men, and partly in the personality of the Teacher, whose living voice carried conviction and presented an inescapable challenge. From the beginning, the portrait of Jesus is of One whose teaching was an integral part of His personality, through which He expressed a message which men might and indeed did repudiate, but which they could not ignore. Apart from His teaching, it is highly unlikely that the opposition to Jesus would have reached the intensity that led to His crucifixion. We cannot separate Jesus from His teaching. As we have reviewed the Beatitudes we have observed repeatedly how what He taught He was. His character was the perfect embodiment of His message, and it is not without significance that in the account of His final commission to His disciples the same word is used and applied to Himself in the splendour of His risen and triumphant majesty as was used earlier in the same gospel to describe the Galilean Teacher: 'He taught them as one having authority'; 'All authority is given to me in heaven and on earth.'

(b) The other question calling for consideration also springs from one of the fruits of Biblical scholarship, namely the importance attached in varying degrees by many scholars to the eschatological element in the gospel – that is to say, the concern of the gospel with the last things or the end of this present world. In the view of not a few, this consideration was dominant, and the teaching of Jesus must be interpreted in the light of it. No one with even a casual knowledge of the New Testament would deny the large place occupied by the Christian hope. It is common ground among all Christians still that the meaning of life is to be understood in relation to it. As at the creation there was a beginning to the world, so there will be an end of it. It may further be recognized that the early Church believed that the end of the present age was imminent. Paul, for example, clearly shared this expectation in the early period of his missionary activity, although he appears to have modified his view later, at any rate to the extent of believing that his own death might precede it. It is uncertain how far our Lord Himself held this view, but quite probably He did so to a considerable extent. It is likely that this coloured much of His teaching. The promises, for example, contained in the Beatitudes may well point the contrast between the present lot of those who practise them and their lot in the good time which He believed to be coming. Indeed the last Beatitude, recognizing the inevitable hardship and persecution attending the faithful disciple in the present state of affairs, and contrasting it with the future reward, suggests that this is so. Sometimes, however, those who hold this eschatological view go further and urge that our Lord's ethical teaching was simply intended as a temporary code, applicable only to the brief period which He expected would precede the end of the present age, and that it has not the same validity in a world where nineteen hundred years have elapsed and the end is not yet. But this attitude to our Lord's teaching overlooks the vital fact that that teaching was rooted in the will of God, and that the warrant for it had nothing whatever to do with the length of time this world would last, but was based on the character of God. We are to behave as sons of the Father, and we are to be perfect because our Father in heaven is perfect. We may indeed go further and affirm that the very fact that we are living in an interval, albeit a much longer interval than our Lord foresaw, reinforces the permanent validity of His teaching. God's character and will are changeless. In eternity His rule prevails; in time that rule was manifested in our Lord Himself, and the blessedness He promised is the blessedness which belongs inalienably to those who accept His rule as their own and live in His Kingdom now. In a similar way, interpretations of the doctrine of eternal life as set forth in the fourth gospel continually remind us that eternal life, though only to be enjoyed in its fulness in the hereafter, is to be entered upon here and now. If the gospel be indeed good news, it must not only bring a message of hope to men concerning their ultimate destiny; it must also speak to their present condition and bring men the power and help they so sorely need.

We have now arrived at a point when, in the light of our examination of the Beatitudes, we may return to the consideration of the place of the teaching of Jesus in the gospel, which is the main theme of this study.

In a book written by a Christian for Christians, it is natural that this theme should have been approached from the religious standpoint. It can with equal relevance be approached from the moral standpoint. Dr A. Macbeath, for example, in his Gifford Lecture 'Experiments in Living', is primarily concerned to establish the autonomy of morality, asserting its independence of religion, but at the same time he is at pains to recognize the intimate connection between the two in the way of mutual influence. 'I am profoundly convinced', he writes, 'that the absence of mutual understanding and support between the saint and the moral and social reformer is a misfortune for both.' On the one hand he stresses the need for the vision of the saint to be transformed into moral energy, for only so will individuals be changed and society transformed; otherwise the vision will grow dim and religion become merely a private luxury or an emotional thrill. On the other hand he urges that, unless the moralist is to lose heart and maybe direction also, the life of moral goodness must be reinforced and sustained by the vision of the saint. Dr Macbeath recalls the conjunction of doing justly and walking humbly in Micah, and expresses grave concern lest, with the growing rift between morality and religion, the decay of religious faith and practice may have a disastrous effect on the very foundations of our way of life.

Such an impressive warning from a leading moral philosopher should surely demonstrate to us, as we approach the issue from the religious angle, the utter inadequacy of any presentation of the gospel which does not find a place for the teaching of our Lord.

In the light of this and of our own examination of the Beatitudes, two opposing interpretations of the significance of Jesus are revealed to be totally inadequate. The first is that held in every age by those who, while rejecting the historic Christian doctrine of the divinity of our Lord and His atoning work, would yet acknowledge the validity of His teaching. Some of them go so far as to deny the existence of God, and many would claim to be agnostics in this respect. But we have already seen that the whole of His teaching springs from His religious insight and is based upon the character of God as revealed by Him. Surely it is manifestly absurd to conclude, as we should be compelled to do if we accepted this view, that the loftiest ethical

teaching the world has ever known, teaching which
has revolutionized man's view of human personality and his standards of conduct, rests on a
fundamental illusion. Such an attitude carries its
own refutation and betrays ignorance of the very
teaching it professes to accept.

The opposite but equally untenable interpretation is that which maintains against all deviations
its faithful adherence to the historic doctrines of
our Lord's person and redemptive work, but
relegates His teaching to a secondary and relatively
unimportant place in the gospel proclamation,
even to the point of suggesting that to stress it is
to fall into the error of humanism. The lamentable
consequence has been that on some occasions in
recent times avowed humanists who reject the
Christian revelation may have shown themselves
more genuinely concerned with the Christian
attitude to the contemporary problems which
baffle mankind than have the representatives of the
Christian Church.

Must we for ever put asunder what God has
joined together? It is Jesus and Jesus alone who
saves. But the Jesus who died for all men on Mount
Calvary and triumphed over death and sin is the
Jesus who proclaimed the way of life on the other
mount in Galilee and said of His teaching, 'Heaven
and earth shall pass away, but my words shall not
pass away.' In Him truth and goodness, religion
and morality find their unique synthesis. They are
revealed to be in essence inseparable. In His life
and in His death, He embodied that eternal goodness of God which in His teaching He had

proclaimed as the way of blessedness for men made in God's image.

This blessedness, which is the fruit of goodness, is not an unattainable goal. It is alike God's demand and His offer; Hence it is an indispensable element in the gospel, which is good news about God and equally good news about man. It reminds us what man is in the intention and purpose of His Creator and Redeemer. One reason that the proclamation of the gospel so often falls on deaf ears today is that it is not presented in a way which seems to meet a need of which men are desperately aware. And yet one of the ironies of the contemporary situation is that man, who has in this generation acquired knowledge in so many fields hitherto unexplored, is unsure of himself. So many secrets, hidden from the beginning of time, have been revealed, but man remains an unsolved enigma. He knows neither whence he came nor whither he goes and consequently he is uncertain what he ought to do and be. Time-honoured moral standards are called into question.

In this plight appeals for conversion seem irrelevant. His primary need is of a moral awakening. The very nature of conversion demands this. Every genuine and lasting evangelical experience must needs be preceded by a moral awakening. John Wesley's moral awakening in 1725 made possible his evangelical experience in 1738. The experiences of moral awakening and evangelical experience need not be separated by a long and painful period of impotence, amounting almost to despair, as happened with Wesley; there are

many well authenticated instances under the
preaching of Wesley himself where the two experiences followed one another during the course of
the same sermon. But a sense of moral need there
must be. Both experiences are equally the result of
God's gracious activity in the human soul.

The present state is sometimes described by
saying that modern man has lost a sense of sin.
This statement needs modifying. He certainly has
an appreciation of the collective failure of mankind,
and concerning himself the prevailing attitude is
not one of claiming perfection but rather one of
fatalistic acceptance of himself as not as good as he
ought to be, unaccompanied by any lively hope
that he can be different. What is really lacking is
not so much a sense of sin as any idea of perfection.

Against this background of resigned despair is
the good news of God in Jesus Christ, setting
forth to men individually and in their relationships
with one another the one way for men and women,
sons and daughters of God, to live in His world,
and offering them in Christ's name the power to
do it. To dismiss the teaching of our Lord as
irrelevant or to shelve it as unpractical is as definite
a rejection of this gospel as would be a denial of
His divinity or His atoning work. Christian
theology and Christian ethics are alike the message
the Church should proclaim. In separation neither
can be effective. The teaching and the redemptive
love of God in Jesus together comprise the challenge and the offer of the eternal God to His
children. If men believe in God at all, they believe

in His willingness to forgive. What never enters into their calculations is that He is both willing and able to make them different, and that here and now His power is available whereby they may bring new life and hope to a world, corrupt and perishing, which is nevertheless a world He made and loves and which He alone can save.